Timeshare Management: The Key Issues for Hospitality Managers

Timeshare Management: The Key Issues for Hospitality Managers

Tammie J. Kaufman
Conrad Lashley
Lisa Ann Schreier

ELSEVIER

AMSTERDAM · BOSTON · HEIDELBERG · LONDON · NEW YORK · OXFORD · PARIS · SAN DIEGO ·
SAN FRANCISCO · SINGAPORE · SYDNEY · TOKYO
Butterworth-Heinemann is an imprint of Elsevier

Butterworth-Heinemann is an imprint of Elsevier

Linacre House, Jordan Hill, Oxford OX2 8DP, UK

30 Corporate Drive, Suite 400, Burlington, MA 01803, USA

First edition 2009

British Library Cataloguing in Publication Data

A catalogue record for this book is available from the British Library

Library of Congress Cataloging-in-Publication Data

A catalog record for this book is available from the Library of Congress

ISBN: 978-0-7506-8599-3

Printed and bound in the United States of America

09 10 10 9 8 7 6 5 4 3 2 1

For information on all Butterwoth-Heinemann
publications visit our website at www.elsevierdirect.com

Working together to grow
libraries in developing countries

www.elsevier.com | www.bookaid.org | www.sabre.org

ELSEVIER   BOOK AID
International   Sabre Foundation

Contents

CHAPTER 13 Vacation Ownership Expansion

Explore the growth of vacation ownership into other segments

Acknowledgments

I would like to thank my family that supported my dreams (Alan, Celeste, Jeff, Julie, Pam, John, Austin, Smylie, Francie, Luckie, and Sarah). I would like to thank my graduate school advisor, Pamela Weaver that molded me kicking and screaming into an academic. I would not be here without her guidance. I would like to thank my chosen family in Orlando that coaxed me along this journey and made me feel that I could accomplish this goal and distracted me when I needed to get away from writing (Kimberly, Randy, Dave, Denver, Duncan, Rose and Bill Jackson, and fortunately for me this list is too long to include everyone). Finally, thank you Conrad and Lisa Ann you have been a terrific team.

Tammie Kaufman

Writing this book has truly been a collaborative effort. Thanks to both Conrad and Tammie for allowing me to contribute and to Sarah, Sunita and everyone at Elsevier for seeing the need for this textbook and their assistance in getting in published. I'd also like to thank those individuals within the timeshare industry who encouraged me to learn and be a catalyst for positive change. On a personal note, thanks to my family and friends for putting up with yet another timeshare endeavour. Finally, to the students and other readers of this textbook may it educate and enlighten you and open up a world of possibilities for you.

Lisa Ann Schreier

FOREWORD

After working through the foreword you should:

- Understand timeshare service

- Recognise the similarities and differences faced by the timeshare sector

- Understand the structure of this book and the approach taken to the study of timeshare services

Understanding Timeshare

Timeshare is a relatively recent business format supporting hospitality and tourism services. Put simply, timeshare formats allow customers to access the right to accommodation within and between countries. The timeshare owner buys accommodation of a certain quality for a given period of time. There are a number of different schemes but the most simple and original format involves the timeshare owner buying the right to stay in particular lodge or apartment in the same resort for a fixed week each year. Rather than buying the lodge or apartment, the timeshare owner buys a part of it which allows them to use the unit for an agreed amount of time each year.

In many ways, the timeshare approach recognises the fears and uncertainties involved in travel, particularly when undertaken internationally. Timeshare enables travellers to return regularly to a place they know and love, and to a property that represents their home away from home. For some it involves holidaying in an area or country from which they originate, but now live permanently elsewhere. For others, timeshare is simply establishing a home from home in a location that is attractive to the owner. Whilst this 'home from home' set of motives are still important for many owners, there has been, over recent years, a growing interest more flexible packages which either do not tie the buyer into a particular location, or are linked to extensive exchange networks which allow owners in one location to swap their weeks to another resort, within countries and across international borders.

As a new business format, the popular image of timeshare has had its ups and downs. In some cases, rogue traders using high pressure selling techniques have created a bad media image of timeshare sales. Complaints from buyers, or would be buyers, about misleading information, and sales presentations that used bullying tactics helped to create an early impression that timeshare was somehow based on a scam or dodgy at best. In response to some of these early concerns, industry in the USA and Europe have set up trade associations which lay down some minimal trading standards to which member companies have to adhere. One important recommendation has been to a minimum 'cooling off' period during which 'would be buyers' are able to formally withdraw from a previously signed agreement. In some cases, individual US states, and the European Union have imposed minimum cooling off periods. In addition to these organisational and legislative attempts to provide more consumer protection, many of the larger hotel companies have now entered the timeshare market. Firms like Marriott, Hilton and De Vere now own considerable portfolios of timeshare properties. Frequently they will develop new sites and resorts with a mixture of hotel and timeshare properties. These firms have pressed for more professional operating standards, as dissatisfied timeshare customers would reflect badly on their hotel operations.

This book aims to provide an introduction to the study of timeshare business operations. It is written with both students and industry practitioners in mind, and focuses on the practical aspects of the timeshare business. The text starts with an overview of the timeshare business, origins and growth as well as developments and trends. It shows that timeshare properties are located in around 100 countries. Ownership is also global, but very much concentrated in just three countries. The USA, Germany and the United Kingdom between are home to over 60 per cent of the world's timeshare owners. The communication chapter follows these chapters which establish ownerships patterns and trends, shows how the patterns of ownership vary and change over time. The next three chapters explore the marketing of timeshare and changes in the approach to marketing timeshare followed by a detail discussion of sales presentations to interested clients. The next three chapters explore some of the practical mechanics in various formats that timeshare can take, together with the role of exchange companies and financing arrangements used by different organisations. Service quality management and the management of human resources, as essential elements of the customer offer, are the subject of the next two chapters. The last two chapters explore variations in the accommodation sector by discussing the development of condominium hotels and other developments in the timeshare model.

As an introductory study in timeshare the book is written in a simple style with some references and academic structures, but these are kept to a minimum. The book is also written in a way that encourages the reader to be actively involved in the reading process. Case studies and concrete examples are provided throughout the book. The use of reflective practise sections also invite the reader to stop and think about the implications of what has just been discussed. Key learning points aim to reinforce learning taking place. The book, therefore, introduces the topic of timeshare, but it also aims to introduce the reader to academic study and style.

The dominant learning style of readers is also one important consideration by the authors. Prior research shows that many of the readers are likely to have a learning style which is know as *Activist* according the work of Honey and Mumford (1983). Without wishing to run through the whole model it is worth reiterating that Activist learners learn best by doing and feeling, and talking with others. They rely more on intuition than on analysis. They need to see the practical application of knowledge. They enjoy here and now activities, such as business games, teamwork tasks and role-plays. They are particularly keen to learn by 'doing', and typically find theoretical approaches difficult. They are attracted to 'people' industries and like active involvement. They work well with others. They will try new ideas. They like variety and excitement. However, they experience difficulties that many experienced educators will recognise. They rarely plan their actions. They rush into answers, and in examination situations may run out of time because they spend too much time on the early questions. They tend not to put effort into topics are not of interest and they often leave things to the last minute.

For the purposes of this book, and for future activities, we suggest that the process of learning needs to move through the stages outline on Kolb's model. Active experience need to be followed by reflection including the critical evaluation of the experience ; and consideration of how these experiences inform or adapt theoretical understanding; and how this might inform future actions, hence, the approach taken in the book. We wish to encourage effective learning by ensuring that the reading process actively engages reflections and critical thinking. We hope, therefore, that the book is instructive and enjoyable,

Conrad Lashley,
Tammie Kaufman,
Lisa Ann Schreier

CHAPTER 1

Vacation Ownership Resort Development: An Overview

After working through this chapter, you should be able to

- Understand the concept of timeshare offer
- Understand that the operations cover a variety of facilities and services
- Recognize that timeshare offers have evolved and changed over time
- Understand that new entrants into the market have increased the professionalism of the sector

INTRODUCTION

The timeshare industry is one of the newest and fastest growing sectors of the international hospitality and tourism experience. Although known as vacation ownership in some quarters, timeshare is the most widely used term to describe the purchase of time periods in locations of choice. The original model involved buying set weeks in a given accommodation in a specific resort, though this model has now been adapted and amended.

The timeshare industry first emerged significantly in Europe in the 1960s. One of the earliest examples emerged in a skiing resort in France. The skiers were wanting to ensure guaranteed accommodation for skiing. Property owners found that they could sell their rights to have access to the same accommodation across the year. Very soon, various US resorts began to sell timeshare weeks in their resorts. Since the 1970s, timeshare has evolved through different international resort locations and resort types, number of resorts, number of owners and variations in the nature of the timeshare offer.

CONTENTS

TIMESHARE EVOLVING

Timeshare evolved as a form of second home ownership with limited rights of access, and also relieved the timeshare owner of the full annual costs of maintaining the property because it is shared with other owners over the year. The term 'timeshare' includes 'time' and 'share' indicating that the approach, in principle, involves sharing time in a given space. Consumer motives and segmentation are discussed more fully in Chapter 2, but since their introduction in skiing villages in France and in Switzerland, time share can be found for a range of resorts across the globe. Table 1.1 lists the different types of resorts in which various forms of timeshare offers are found. Each resort offers a number of different benefits which are likely to appeal to differing lifestyles.

In fact, the first timeshare operation was begun in the 1950s in Europe by a Swiss company known as Hapimag. They sold shares in their hotel and used the proceeds to buy holiday accommodation across Europe. The 'shareholders' had the right to use these properties on a regular basis.

- The benefits to the shareholder are that they can get regular access to properties which they know and trust.

- They are aware of the quality and service standards, as well as the location.

- The hotelier is able to raise capital with which to expand.

- The hotelier overcomes problems relating to accommodation – the space is sold even if the individual timeshare does not materialise that year.

Table 1.1 Timeshare Resort Types
Resort Type
Seaside/ocean
Regional
Golf
Snow/ski
Lake/river
Urban
Theme park
Casino/gambling
Other

Source: Ernst & Young, 2006:15

In the 1970s, US property developers were going through a crisis and were looking for innovative ways to sell properties. The fact that they were selling properties in a way that opened up property purchase to a larger number of people meant that there were more buyers. They had to increase and change marketing and sales activities, because they were now selling the same apartment 52 times each week of the year. Most importantly, they released the capital value of the property for further property development.

> **Key point 1.1**
> Timeshare evolved in the latter part of the twentieth century to provide a form of holiday resort ownership based on the purchase of time periods.

At a similar time, timeshare owners in the US began to swap and exchange visits to different resorts, first on an informal basis, but later this resulted in the formation of Resort Condominiums International (RCI) as an organization devoted to enabling exchanges. Later, Interval International (II) was created also enabling exchanges of weeks and resorts among timeshare owners.

> **Reflective practice 1.1**
> **a]** Consider what the strengths and weaknesses of owning a timeshare property might be.
> **b]** Consider the strengths and weaknesses from the resort developer's perspective.

Independently of these developments in the USA, timeshare began to develop in the UK, France, Italy and in Scandinavia. Initially, the majority of sales were to British citizens buying properties in their favourite resort destinations in Spain. Europe is now the second largest timeshare market in the world after the USA. Table 1.2 provides an overview of estimates of the world market based on the number of resorts.

The point to note here is that these figures are taken for slightly different time periods, as it is difficult to get hold of accurate up-to-date figures for global timeshare resorts, and even the European figures are somewhat out of date. However, they do show that the majority of timeshare resorts are located in the USA and Europe, and that most timeshare owners are located in the same two continents. Using these figures, 70 per cent of timeshare resorts are located in the USA or in Europe and the OTE (2002: 9) states that some 74 percent are resident in the two continents.

Table 1.2 Estimates of the Number of Timeshare Resorts

Global Number of Resorts	Resorts Based in the USA	Resorts Based in Europe
4325	1604	1452

Source: see Chapter 2, Table 2.1

In the early stages, most timeshare development companies were independents, and sales techniques were not always ethical. High pressure selling, and some instances of fraudulent selling meant that the industry developed a dodgy reputation. However, this began to change when some of the larger property development and international hotel chains began to enter the market. Table 1.3 lists some of the recent entrants into the timeshare market in Europe.

As more corporate players have entered the field, there has been an increasing concern to tidy up the trading practices of timeshare operators. Sales techniques in particular have been a major focus. Allowing a cooling-off period between the sales presentation and acceptance and final confirmation has been a particular concern in many countries. The OTE's *Code of Ethics* requires all members to build in a period between signing a contract to purchasing a timeshare interval, and the agreement becoming binding; typically in the EU this is about 10 days. In the USA, this is called '*Rescission rights*', that is, the right to withdraw from a signed contract within a fixed period.

Both the *American Resort Development Association* and the *Organization Timeshare Europe* have developed codes of practice binding on members. Apart from the requirements for 'rescission periods' or cooling-off

Table 1.3 Recent Entrants into the Timeshare Market

Timeshare Companies	Main Business	Country of Origin
Barratt Group	Property developer	Britain
Metro Group	Supplies and property	Germany
Club Mediterrannee	Resorts	France
Berlusconi Group	Conglomerate	Italy
Sol Hotel Group	Hotels	France
Hilton	Hotels	Britain/USA
De Vere Group	Hotels	UK
Disney	Resorts	USA
TUI	Resorts	Britain

period most of these codes tread a line between trying not to stifle genuine entrepreneurial activity and protecting potential owners from high pressure or dishonest selling. In principle, they offer a code of conduct which sets baseline standards to protect reputable firms from the antics of some rogue traders but which do not restrict *free enterprise*. Hence, they are almost exclusively concerned with the protection of potential timeshare owners and rarely consider other interest groups such as employees, or the local communities in which resorts are located (Upchurch & Lashley, 2007).

Key point 1.2

As timeshare has grown, trade bodies have developed to represent the sector and these bodies have developed codes of practice protecting consumer interests which are binding on their members.

THE EVOLVING TIMESHARE SERVICE

In the early stages, time share owners bought a fixed week in a fixed property unit (fully appointed luxury apartment, villa, cottage or suite) for a fixed week(s) in high, medium, or low season bands in a given resort. This is described in Table 1.4 as 'Fixed unit/fixed interval'.

Over the years, more flexibility has been built into the offer to consumers.

- The '**Fixed unit/float interval**' involves purchase of a time period in a fixed unit, but this might float with regard to week(s) taken, though these are likely to be taken at high, medium or low season.

- In some cases, timeshare owners buy a set period of time but are not tied into availing themselves of that period in the same unit, or in the same resort. These are referred to as a '**Float unit/fixed interval**' in the table.

Table 1.4	Variations in the Timeshare Arrangement

Fixed unit/fixed interval
Fixed unit/float interval
Float unit/fixed interval
Fixed unit/float season
Float unit/float season
Points

Source: Ernst & Young, 2006:15

- A small number of timeshare relationships (see Chapter 2) involve having access to a fixed unit in different seasons. Typically, the purchase of a high season week may result in access to several weeks in the low season – referred to as a '**Fixed unit/float season**' in Table 1.4.

- One of the more flexible arrangements for owners involves a '**Float unit/float season**' whereby the arrangement allows timeshare owners to vary between units, resorts and seasons.

- Finally, the ultimately flexible offer allows for the consumer to buy enough '**points**' to meet vacation needs. Disney was one of the first to introduce the vacation club based on the purchase of points. This allows the timeshare owner to purchase enough points to vary the accommodation size in bedrooms or in seasons, or number of weeks used.

Reflective practice 1.2

a] Consider the strengths and weaknesses of each of the above arrangements from the timeshare consumer's perspective.

b] How might these arrangements suit the needs of different kinds of timeshare consumers?

c] Consider the strengths and weaknesses from the resort developer's perspective.

Key point 1.3

The timeshare offer to consumers has evolved over time as some consumers have asked for more flexibility in the timeshare experience.

EVOLVING LEGAL APPROACHES

Given the somewhat unusual nature of the timeshare unit purchaser and the resort owner, a number of models for handling the legal relationship have emerged. The three most common types of conveyance are (a) deeded interests, (b) right to use, and (c) leasehold agreements.

1] Under a **deeded interest** method of conveyance, the purchaser receives a title for the real property that is being purchased from the timeshare developer. The unit owner, in effect, buys the right to use that unit (apartment, etc.) in perpetuity. Like any bought object, it is the owner's rights to use it in perpetuity, sell it on and pocket the proceeds and leave it to others as part of the estate, when the owner dies. In effect, the resort developer sells the ownership of various time periods for each unit.

2] The **right-to-use** type of conveyance is not associated with deeding of the underlying real property to the purchaser; instead, the individual is given contractual rights to use the timeshare facilities for a specified period of time. Usually, this would involve the interval purchased, say one week, but for time periods limited in the agreement, say 25 years.

3] A **leasehold agreement** is similar to a right-to-use contract in that the purchaser holds a leasehold interest or other interest of less than a full ownership interest. In practical terms, this means that the purchaser has the right to inhabit the timeshare unit for a specified period of time, and at the termination of the lease, the property reverts to the timeshare developer. Typically, the time period concerned is shorter than with a right-to-use agreement.

Irrespective of the precise legal nature of the agreement, in effect the time-share consumer is usually known as the owner. Any given developer can build and sell an individual unit for 51 or 52 weeks out of a year, depending on whether a week is held out for general maintenance purposes. Timeshare offers are unique in both the hospitality and tourism sector and the property ownership sector. In hotels, and in the accommodation sector, individuals pay to use the unit for a specific time period, but this does not imply ownership nor does it enable the guest to claim user rights over the same time period.

Key point 1.4

A timeshare owner's legal rights to the property vary according to the nature of the contract established at the point of the initial sale. Not all agreements allow the owner to sell or bequeath the property to heirs.

EXCHANGE SERVICES

Whilst there are clearly different motives for owning a timeshare interval (see Chapter 2) many owners are attracted to timeshare ownership because there are opportunities to exchange their interval at one of a number of national or international resorts. Paradoxically, timeshare owners are buying the right to access another home, but many do not want to be tied down to just one location. That said, there are many who like the idea of returning to the same location in the same week each year. However, for many, the exchange allows the purchaser of one vacational period in a given resort for the use of a vacant accommodation owned by someone at another time and/ or in another resort.

In most cases, a resort when developed becomes affiliated with one of the major exchange companies which organizes the exchange transactions for resort owners. In most resorts, this opportunity to exchange the bought location and time period for another location or time period is the fundamental aspect of the offer. In fact, most developers will pay for the first year of a two-year membership of the exchange company.

Two major organizations dominate the global vacation (timeshare) exchange business:

- II is based in Miami, FL, and

- RCI has headquarters offices in Carmel, IN, and Parsippany, NJ.

RCI is the bigger organization with more affiliated resorts, consumers serviced, a larger stock of weeks, as well as a larger number of confirmed exchanges (ARDA, 2002). Collectively, these two exchange companies service almost 6000 resorts with over four million members worldwide (ARDA, 2002:181).

The exchange system allows timeshare owners to potentially trade their interval for a similar interval in another resort within the exchange organization's books. Vacant units are not automatically made available to exchange; the owner must formally put them in the company's list of week available. The exchange companies base their charges on entering the registry. Charges are only made when there is take-up of that unit and that week at that resort. The transaction fee (in addition to a membership fee) is only charged when the exchange service is performed. Under a point system, the interval is put into a programme which allows the member (typically club members) to exchange the points purchased in a number of ways.

These exchange organizations do not own resorts. II and RCI affiliate resorts apply to be members into an exchange network. Given that the ability to exchange the interval is a potential added benefit for many would-be timeshare buyers, resort developers sign up their resorts to one or, in a few cases, both of the exchange agencies. In addition, resort managers automatically enrol all buyers in one or in some cases both of the exchange agencies.

> **Key point 1.5**
> Recognizing that many timeshare owners are interested in exchanging their timeshare experiences, II and RCI have developed as the major international timeshare exchange agencies.

RESALE

The issue of resale has been something of a complicated matter, and highly dependent on the legal format of the timeshare arrangement, as discussed earlier. Under the deed of covenant or fee simple arrangement, the owner has the right to sell the ownership like any purchased property. Under the right-to-use arrangement or vacation club (points), no such right may exist. The initial contract of agreement should clarify the position about resale. Under most codes of conduct, the sales person is required to clarify these resale rights, or limitations. ARDA (2002:196) suggests the following as to why timeshare (vacation) owners may want to sell.

1] *Lifestyle change:* death, retirement, change in family circumstances, illness, retirement, change of residential location, children growing up and moving away.

2] *Owner's death:* This may be necessary to liquidate the owner's assets.

3] *Maintenance fee and other assessments:* Owners believe that these ongoing costs of maintaining access to the timeshare property are too high and beyond their current financial resources.

4] *Dissatisfaction with the product:* It may be that the purchase and/or the resort has not lived up to expectations.

5] *Profit making:* Where the owners can see the growing popularity of the resort is increasing the market value of the properties in the resort, they may decide to liquidate the value of the unit and take the profit.

Clearly the most important barrier to resale is the level of demand for ownership of properties in the resort. Alongside the level of maintenance of the property this will impact on the perceived value of the unit in comparison to the purchase price. A well-maintained property in a highly sought after resort will maintain if not increase its resale value and the number of potential buyers.

> **Key point 1.6**
> The right to resell the property is a function of the initial agreement. Where the right exists, timeshare owners have the same rights to transfer ownership as with any other property.

RESORT MANAGEMENT

The resort developer usually handles the early stages of the resort development, whilst the property is still being developed and the selling process is in the initial phase. After these initial contacts with the resort sales and marketing team, the owner's main contacts are with the resort's property management company. There are three basic formats:

1] The resort developer can manage the resort properties with a contractual agreement with the resorts 'timeshare owners association'.

2] The timeshare owners association may contract an outside firm to manage the resort and maintain the properties.

3] The timeshare owners may decide to manage the property internally.

Whichever of these formats is employed, the key focus of the actions is to ensure that individual properties are kept to their original standard and that wider resort facilities are both maintained and developed in line with the resort owner's expectations and needs. Within the unit, the maintenance budget will be used to keep the décor up to the standard, equipment serviced and replaced, as well as maintain all furnishings. Given the potential change in owners though sales, and the need to attract existing owners to use the resort as well as attract them from other resorts that are exchanging into the resort, the development and enhancement of facilities is highly important.

The responsibilities of the timeshare maintenance organization are likely to include the following:

- *The operation of the resort:* This would include employing personnel responsible for hospitality services, housekeeping, recreation and leisure activities, food and beverage facilities, shops, etc. In other words, this ensures that the property functions as a resort.

■ *Maintenance and upkeep of the property:* This would be a programme of planned maintenance of the individual units as well as of the resort. This ensures that individual units are in full working order before each interval.

In addition, the association undertakes all the budgeting and financial management necessary to ensure that the resort continues to be maintained and developed along the lines agreed upon with the timeshare owners. Typically, the association is controlled collectively by the timeshare owners, and an annual general meeting of timeshare owners helps set the agenda for the forthcoming year, reviews the activities of the previous year, generally holds the management team top account.

> **Key point 1.6**
> After the early stages of development, management of the resort usually passes on to some third party. There are a variety of arrangements, but the management is typically independent of the resort development, most frequently a body managed by the timeshare owners as a group.

MOVEMENTS AND DEVELOPMENTS

The timeshare product, as represented by the property built and sold on to the timeshare owner, has been through significant evolution and change. Increasing demand from consumers has been, without doubt, a major influence on designers and resort developers. Would-be owners have been increasing their expectations of the quality of the final fit and the configuration of the accommodation in each unit. That said, the developers themselves, have been instrumental in increasing the quality and luxury of fit as a means of securing a competitive advantage. In addition, the various regulatory bodies in the form of trade bodies, and national and local governments have had a hand in influencing resort development design.

Property design demands

In the 1970s, many resorts were built around a two bedroom, two bathroom format. Typically, resort developers were dealing in family formats, and campus style resort settings. Later, these changed into more luxurious suites, and the industry began to look to other segments for the design of accommodation. Golfers, for example, will be happy with accommodation which requires two couples, though they often require twin beds, so as to maximize flexibility. Accommodation packages for some market segments are now including three and four bedroom properties, though the nature of the resort and the occasionality most used will have an impact on the way the accommodation is configured. The growth in the number of residential units coincides with the size of the individual unit from less than 100 square feet to over 2000 square feet per unit per villa.

The standard configuration for these early campus style structures was the two to three level condo style structures with surrounding onsite recreational activities. The campus style of timeshare resorts in the 21st century has gravitated towards townhouses and single-family units with individual pools. So customers are more interested in owning a property that symbolically represents a second home.

The scale of development has changed considerably over the years. In the 1970s, a resort would typically be considered to be developed if it has about 50 units. Nowadays, resorts may have as many as 900–1000 units. In some cases, they may contain properties built for timeshare ownership, as well as a luxury hotel. The economies of scale allow more facilities and services to be offered to both timeshare and hotel guests. So larger resorts, attracting larger footfall will offer more choices in restaurant and bar facilities, as well as a greater range of leisure resources.

In addition to this multi-unit site, developers may aim to stage the financing and construction of units. Typically, they would be built in phases, and the next phase of construction does not commence until 50 per cent of the timeshare property capacity has been sold. Apart from the obvious advantage of building the next of buildings with capital raised from the sale of the earlier properties, the sale of units was slower than the time taken to build them. Sometimes, the configuration of properties constructed assumes that some properties will be sold for long-term use and these might be constructed first. Typically, property let out for a short-term and for timeshare would be constructed later.

Properties built for overseas consumers may be larger as many who tend to stay for three to four weeks will require more space for luggage and personal effects. For example, as many visitors to some of the US beach resorts live overseas, individual units are bigger.

Bearing in mind the need to both attract timeshare owners and keep owners art the resort, rather than exchanging their week at the resort for another resort, resort developers have an interest in creating resort amenities which leave a lasting impression. Amenities vary according to the type of resort, the land available and the profile of the typical customer. These might include all the facilities of a leisure club – indoor and outdoor swimming pools, gymnasium, sauna and steam-room facilities, massage and beauty therapy facilities, as well as horse riding and pony trekking, boating and marina facilities, on-site shopping, various gourmet dining facilities, theatre and club facilities in addition to guided tours and transport facilities to local attractions.

Evolving industry standards

Whilst the growth of consumer demand enforced an important increase in expectations of property size, finish and design, the entry of some of the major branded hotel and resort companies into the resort development market had an impact. Companies such as Marriott, DeVere, Hilton, Hyatt and Disney increased property quality because they had vested interest in protecting their name and improving the quality service experience of their visitors. Their experiences of the benefits of standardization and trading credibility meant that they became vociferous advocates for improving standards.

Perhaps more importantly, however, the two major exchange agencies, RCI and II, began rating resorts as a way of better informing their customers wishing to use their exchange services. These systems classify resorts based on particulars such as ease of guest flow, presence of private sleeping areas, bathrooms that are accessible without walking through the bedroom; kitchen amenities are specified based on the size of the unit, and other amenities are specified as mandatory (e.g., partial or full kitchen, with a coffeemaker, small refrigerator, microwave, oven, and a four-burner stove. In addition, wet bars, larger televisions, or VCRs, depending on the unit and market.

The important point is that these point rating systems give customers a means to evaluate the resorts they might be considering as exchange locations; also it influences the potential selling price of the intervals being sold at different resorts. Resort developers and resort maintenance associations now have material interest in keeping the quality rating at a high level, as this has an impact on initial purchase rates, as well as on the interest from would-be exchange clients.

> **Key point 1.7**
> Over recent decades, the size and quality of timeshare units have evolved and the size of resorts has increased. These changes are driven by consumers, the involvement and named hospitality industry brands as well as by the rating of resorts according to their facilities and services on offer.

SUMMARY

Timeshare, or vacation, ownership involves an emerging array of different products and services. Traditionally, timeshare meant the purchase of the ownership of a unit for an agreed interval. In other words, this means buying the apartment, or villa, for a period of time, typically sold in set weeks over the year. A timeshare owner bought the right to use the same unit for the same period each year. Over the last few decades, an increasing number of timeshare owners have wanted to exchange access to their property for access to other properties. This resulted in the emergence of organizations such as the RCI and II specializing in the organization of exchanges. Subsequently, this has resulted in increasingly flexible arrangements where the owner could change either weeks, or units, or even both. The most flexible arrangement is in vacation clubs where owners buy points which can be translated into different kinds of properties and time slots.

Apart from changes in the design of individual units and resorts, the timeshare sector has been influenced by a number of actors and agencies. The emergence of the RCI and II has greatly aided the exchange of intervals and time slots giving owners more choice in their timeshare experience. These two organizations have been instrumental in enhancing the quality of timeshare products and services and through their ranking of resorts according to the quality provided. In addition, the increasing involvement of major hospitality accommodation providers has increased demands to improve the trading standards in the sector. This in turn has resulted in the American Resort Development Association and Organization Timeshare Europe being two leading trade associations for the sector.

CHAPTER 2

The Vacation Owner

After working through this chapter, you should be able to

- understand different techniques for segmenting timeshare customers
- identify current timeshare customer profiles
- discuss models for understanding customer behaviour
- identify the various motives for timeshare ownership

INTRODUCTION

Although timeshare ownership is a global phenomenon with owners originating from every inhabited continent, ownership is not evenly spread through the world's population. Timeshare owners originate more frequently from a narrow range of countries. They have a limited demographic profile with different age and social class profiles than the population as a whole. They do not have a single motive for purchasing timeshare experiences. It is important to understand the profiles and motives of those making timeshare purchases so that promotional and sales efforts can be better and more effectively focused on.

This chapter explores some of the dominant characteristics of those who are owners of timeshare packages, and it puts forward two dominant techniques. The first describes timeshare consumers via their demographic profile, their age, position in life, family profile and national origins. The second considers the occasionality being connected when making

CONTENTS

a timeshare related purchase. Occasionality is concerned with reasons as to why purchasers buy into timeshare. In effect, the same consumers may buy into different timeshare packages because these packages deliver different timeshare benefits.

TIMESHARE LOCATIONS

Timeshare resorts are predominantly located in major vacation resorts. Table 2.1 gives the latest figures for locations of timeshare resorts, at the time of writing, in Europe and the USA. These data show that timeshare resorts are highly concentrated in both regions. In the USA, Florida has the largest number of resorts – over 25 per cent of the nation's resorts are in that state. In Europe, Spain has 35 per cent of all of Europe's timeshare resorts. Although to date international data are difficult to come by, ARDA's (2003) study suggested that there were 4325 resorts worldwide, and that timeshare resorts located in Europe and in the USA accounted for 70 per cent of all timeshare resorts. Between them, Spain in Europe and Florida in the USA account for over 20 per cent of the timeshare resorts.

Table 2.1	European and US Timeshare Resort Profile				
Aggregate Resort Profile		**Key European Locations***		**US State Profile****	
Location	Frequency	Location	Frequency	Location	Frequency
Worldwide	4325	Europe	1452	USA	1604
		Spain	512	Florida	378
		Italy	186		
		France	142	California	123
		UK	139	South Carolina	117
		Portugal	124	Hawaii	92
		Austria	55		
		Greece	45	Colorado	77
		Turkey	38	North Carolina	55
		Germany	38	Nevada	60
		Switzerland	37	Missouri	49
		Finland	31	Texas	54
		Malta	23	All others	553

Source: *Organization Timeshare Europe (2001), The European Timeshare Industry in 2001, London
**Ernst & Young (2006), State of the Vacation Timeshare Industry: US study, ARDA International Foundation

Key learning point 2.1

Timeshare resorts are primarily located in certain geographical areas. The USA and Europe account for over 70 per cent of all timeshare resorts, with Florida and Spain being major locations.

Although mainly located in Europe and in the USA, timeshare resorts are found in 81 countries (OTE, 2001), in Asia, Australia/Oceania, Africa, the Caribbean, Central America, the Middle East, South America and other parts of North America (Upchurch & Lashley, 2006). In fact, international timeshare resort sales were reported to be equivalent to $9.4 billion in 2002.

The total number of timeshare units per resort has grown over the years as timeshare products have evolved. In the USA, the average number of units (apartments, etc.) was 27 per resort in 1975; by 1990, the figure had grown to 56 units per resort, and by 2006, it was 96 per resort (Ernst & Young, 2006). In Europe, the average number of units was 57 per resort, but this ranges from 249 per resort in the Netherlands and nine per resort in Ireland (OTE, 2001).

Types of resorts

Timeshare resorts can be seen to be located in a number of different settings. Seaside or ocean resorts are the most popular (Ernst & Young, 2006), followed by regional resorts, and golf resorts. Table 2.2 lists the locations by types of resorts as reported in the latest US study (Ernst & Young, 2006). The

Table 2.2 US resort's Primary Characteristics

Resort Type	Percentage of Resorts Responding
Seaside/ocean	31.9
Regional	13.7
Golf	10.2
Snow/ski	9.3
Lake/river	9.0
Urban	6.0
Theme park	5.3
Casino/gambling	2.1
Other	12.5
Total	100

Source: Ernst & Young (2006:15)

survey asked timeshare resort manager respondents to identify the primary characteristics of their timeshare resorts.

The OTE report (2001) shows that European countries differ in the way they offer the setting for resort locations. Spain, for example, has the largest number of resorts, 512 at the time of the study. Of these, 90.7 per cent were in beach locations, whereas the UK with 129 resorts had only 16.8 in beach locations and 50.4 per cent resorts in rural locations. Not surprisingly, Switzerland had no beach resorts, but it had 45.2 per cent ski resorts, and the remaining 37 resorts were located on mountains or in lake areas.

Key learning point 2.2

Timeshare varies across different countries in regard to where key locations are found.

Timeshare products

The traditional service marketing literature suggests offers to service consumers. The seven 'P's represent the benefits to customers that flow from a service offer. These are listed in Table 2.3.

Each timeshare resort develops an offer to customers related to these seven P's. **Product:** In timeshare, the nature of the actual accommodation units in the form of the apartment or lodge constitutes the core element of the product that is being purchased by the customer. **Price:** The timeshare price consists of a number of elements – the purchase of the time in the unit, the additional service charges, and additional prices of leisure facilities, meals in restaurants, green fees, etc. The price level is assumed to communicate service quality. **Place:** Even though many timeshare owners use the services of exchange companies, there are many whose purchase is solely linked to a key location. **Promotion:** This is useful for focusing on media likely to be

Table 2.3	The Service Marketing Mix as Applied to Timeshare
Product	
Price	
Place	
Promotion	
People	
Processes	
Premises	

Table 2.4	Resort Use Plan	Percentage of Resorts Responding
Fixed unit/fixed interval		39.0
Fixed unit/float interval		6.2
Float unit/fixed interval		2.3
Fixed unit/float season		0.8
Float unit/float season		21.0
Points		30.7
Total		100

Source: Ernst & Young (2006:15)

used by the key market segments of customers. **People:** The interaction of various personnel with customers is also part of the offer to customers and shapes their evaluation of resort operators. **Processes:** The availability of flexibility arrangements for changing weeks within the primary resort and the ease with which it is possible to exchange the arrangement with another similar resort are also important features of the timeshare marketing mix. **Premises:** The overall décor, property configuration in the form of bedrooms, en-suite facilities, living space, quality of fixtures and fittings have to be consistent with the brand. All service offers to customers, including a range of timeshare offers, can be analysed according to this seven P model.

Reflective practice 2.1

[a] Compare two businesses offering a similar product or service but offering differing marketing mixes to their customers, for example, two hotels, two restaurants or two bars.

[b] Think about how different timeshare resorts might vary in the marketing mix offered to customers – try and compare a beach location with a golf location.

Over the years, timeshare offers to customers have evolved, and now timeshare customers have a number of ways of engaging with the timeshare experience. These timeshare plans which are outlined in the Ernst & Young report (2006) are listed in Table 2.4. The traditional and original model is the most popular. That is where the timeshare owner buys a set time period within a set property unit. This is closely followed by the point system in which timeshare customers buy a set number of points and redeems these against properties and times of the year, as they see fit.

Table 2.5	Affiliations/Exchange Programs	Percentage of Resorts Responding
Interval international and/or RCI		93.6
ICE		22.5
Self-administered		9.9
Other		4.9

Source: Ernst & Young (2006:15)

Those who have fixed units or fixed resorts have often required assistance in finding alternative locations, or in letting out their unit if they are unable to visit that week or interval, or they cannot visit the resort for some reason. Most timeshare resorts involve the work of specialist firms that organize swaps or find people interested in taking on units for a desired period. There are in effect two major organizations, RCI and Interval International, which most respondents identified in the Ernst & Young study (2006) as being indicated by 93.6% of respondents. Table 2.5 highlights the exchange organizations with their potential share of the market as indicated by respondents in the survey. Multiple responses were allowed because some respondents would be with a number of different exchange organizations. ICE specialize in cruise exchange programmes, whilst just under 10 per cent of resorts handle the exchange programme themselves.

Key learning point 2.3

Most timeshare owners affiliate with one or other of the big exchange programmes so as to enable exchanges.

TIMESHARE MARKET SEGMENTATION

Much sales promotion is often directed at potential customers who are unsuitable and unlikely to purchase timeshare products. In fact, timeshare owners represent a narrow sector of the total population. Their age profile, position in life, family relationship, and country of origin are all features where the timeshare owner differs from the core population. There is a need to draw a clear picture of what timeshare owners are like and to think about offering sales and promotional activities in a way that is most appealing.

There are two principle ways to describe customers: The first describes them via their demographic profile, that is, describing timeshare owners according to socio-economic position, age, sex, family life cycle stage, and where appropriate country of origin. The second method segments customers according to occasionality, that is, looking at the motives for making a purchase decision. The same customer may make very different purchase decisions on the basis of different assessment of needs.

Demographic segmentation

The demographic profile of an individual or a household is developed by asking a certain number of questions which are summarized in Table 2.6. The *socio-economic* profile is concerned with a combination of economic and social factors relating to the type of work done, the social class, and the economic standing. To some extent, these issues overlap, but not always completely. Life-cycle position relates to the stage in a person or a household's life. The model assumes a series of stages in their typical lives. Each stage represents a series of features, including freedom, family structure and likely constraints. Gender is concerned with the sex of the purchaser or purchase decision maker. Gender can cause individuals to respond to different sales messages or features of the marketing mix in different ways. Geographical features, relate typically to the type of housing and area in which an individual or household reside. These features describe whether an area consists of privately owned homes, or rented properties, or of new or old housing, and provide an insight into resources available to the purchaser.

Lifestyle features relate to the individual or households drives and aspirations. These might shape their concerns when making a purchase or prioritize some features of the marketing mix over others. Finally, personality features in terms of extroversion/introversion can be influential in shaping consumption priorities and sales messages which are most appealing.

Globally, there are estimated to be 10.7 million timeshare properties. Ernst and Young's report claims that there were 4.1 million US households that are timeshare owners. According to the OTE report, it is difficult to accurately calculate the number of owners in Europe, but they estimate 1.4 million in Europe (OTE, 2001; Table 2.7). They estimate that 48 per cent of all timeshare owners are based in the USA, and 31 per cent live in Europe. Within Europe, the UK and Germany account for over 50 per cent of all European timeshare ownership (TRI Consulting, 2002).

Interval Internationals Membership profile (Simmons, 2006) shows that the average US timeshare owner member is around 50 years of age, is married and lives in a three-person household. They appear to be one and a half times more likely to be married than the general US adult populations and one and a half times as likely to fall into the 45–64 year age group.

Table 2.6	Demographic Characteristics
Socio-economic group	*Income and status groups* A Professional – doctors, senior managers B Intermediate – middle managers, teachers C1 White collar – clerical staff, administrative staff C2 Skilled manual – artisans, engineers D Unskilled – routine job holders, service providers/product manufacturers E Low income – unemployed, pensioners
Life cycle position	*People in different stages of life* Bachelor stage Newly married – no children Full nest I (child under 6) Full nest II (child over 6) Full nest III (dependent older children) Empty nest I (no children family head working) Empty nest II (family head retired) Solitary survivor (working) Solitary survivor (retired)
Gender	Male Female Gay men Gay women
Geographical	A classification of residential networks (ACORN) Divides people according to the area in which they live: 17 groups and 54 neighbourhood types
Life style	Based on educational, income, occupation, social contact, and individual preferences, e.g. – environmentally aware – health conscious – materialistic
Personality	Extrovert–introvert Stable–unstable Tough minded–tender minded

A European study (OTE, 2001) shows that a very high proportion of timeshare owners have no children in their family. This incidence does vary by country, but as a rule, between half and three quarters of timeshare owners do not have children. Table 2.8 reports on the profile of Interval International owners.

The average income for the Interval International customers at $139,800 is reckoned to be more than double that of the average US household. Thirty

Table 2.7	Analysis of European Timeshare Ownership by Current Residence of the Owner	
Country of Residence	**Number of Owners (000's)**	**Percentage of all Owners**
UK	441.8	31.6
Germany	282.6	20.6
France	103.0	7.3
Italy	93.2	6.7
Spain	67.4	4.8
Finland	57.8	4.1
Austria	33.3	2.4
Switzerland	32.2	2.1
Netherlands		

Source: Adapted from OTE Report (2001:50)

Table 2.8	Age, Gender, Marital Status, and Household Size in the Interval International Study		
	Interval 2003 (%)	**Interval 2006 (%)**	**US Population 2006 (%)**
Marital status			
Single (never married)	5.1	5.6	23.4
Married	83.7	80.0	57.8
Separated/divorced	8.2	9.7	12.4
Widowed	3.0	4.7	6.4
Household size			
1	13.3	10.2	14.1
2	45.8	49.5	38.8
3–4	33.2	29.9	34.2
5 or more	7.7	10.4	12.9
Mean	2.7	2.7	2.8
Median	2.0	2.0	–

Source: Simmons (2006)

five per cent of members earn between $50,000 and $100,000, and 25 per cent report incomes in excess of $150,000. In addition, Interval's members are three times more likely to reckon that they have household incomes in excess of $250,000.

The American Resort Association report that timeshare owners tend to be within a specific age band and have a higher than average income. The largest owner age group is within the 35–55 year old age band, and almost 80% have an income over $50,000 (ARDA, 2002). Of these, 64% have a college degree and 31% have a post-graduate degree, demonstrating a profile that suggests a more qualified, and therefore a more professional profile amongst owners. Certainly, timeshare owners are more likely to be from the professional and managerial socio-economic groups. Of US timeshare owners, 85% are married with children, confirming the 'Full-nest' category in various stages.

European timeshare owners typically have no children at home and most likely have an 'empty nest' (TRI, 2001), a picture further supported by the age of timeshare owners in Europe. Most of the new owners are between 40 and 60 years (TRI, 2001:52), and this age group makes up 40–50% of all owners. Although the majority of owners can be described as middle aged, married and from the higher socio-economic groups, ARDA (2002) suggest that there are significant ownership segments amongst single person households, and retirees.

In Europe, the profile has some interesting variations when compared within European ownership and in comparison with US timeshare ownership. Table 2.9 shows that amongst the two key ownership countries – Germany and the UK – most owners are couples without children living at home.

The OTE study confirmed that European timeshare owners were more likely to have taken on multiple ownerships. Nearly 80 per cent of all European owners had taken on multiple ownership. The average for all countries was 1.75 weeks per owner. A very high proportion of European timeshare owners had no children living at home. There are some national variations, but between one half and three quarters of the timeshare owning households from individual countries have no children at home. They say, 'Broadly speaking timeshare has not established itself as a family pursuit' (OTE, 2001:52). In most cases, between 45 and 50 per cent of new timeshare owners are aged between 40 and 60 years. They also report that in the UK,

Table 2.9	Number in Each Owning Family in the Top Five of European Timeshare Owning Nations				
Number of Children in Household	UK (%)	Germany (%)	France (%)	Italy (%)	Spain (%)
None	70.3	67.9	56.7	50.7	43.3
One	13.3	16.5	18.9	27.3	29.6
Two	12.7	121.8	16.9	18.8	24.1
Three	2.9	2.2	5.3	18.8	24.1
Four	0.6	0.3	1.5	2.8	2.7
Five	0.1	0	0.4	0.1	0.1
Six	0.1	0	0.3	0	0

Source: Adapted from OTE Report (2001:50)

France and Sweden, over 20 per cent of new timeshare owners are aged between 60 and 70 years.

Key learning point 2.4

Although there are some national variations, most timeshare owners are drawn from a narrow band of the global population.

Reflective practice 2.2

[a] Using the features outlined in Table 2.6, describe the demographic profile of most timeshare owners.

[b] Contrast and compare US owners with European owners.

Segmentation by occasionality

Increasingly, hospitality and tourism retailers are defining and developing their brands around the occasions that customers use their type of business. To some extent, this breaks out of the somewhat constrained way of segmenting customers by the demographic characteristics outlined in Table 2.6. In recent years, it has been recognized that the same customer may visit the same premises for different reasons and at different times of the week. Crucially, the customer's definition of what makes the visit a success will be different. The critical success factors by which the customer evaluates the quality of the visit will differ. For example, the same customer may go to restaurants for several different eat-out occasions. Customers might be eating to *refuel* whilst working or shopping; because they *can't be bothered to* cook and eat out as a replacement; to celebrate a *special occasion* to mark a birthday or an anniversary; or for a *family meal out* (Lashley & Lincoln, 2002).

Although the occasions are different for the timeshare sector, the concept can be harnessed by timeshare operators. The key benefit is that it helps the operator to think more clearly about why the customer is making this particular timeshare purchase, the features that will be expected for an evaluation of success and the benefits being sought There exist potential conflicts with other customers when there are contradictory occasions. This latter point is crucial because some accessions may involve conflictual differences between customers making purchase decisions for different occasions.

Home from home occasions

The home from home occasion chiefly concerns having a base that is perceived as their space and their 'second home'. Customers buy into timeshare because they have a need for a sense of permanence and belonging to a specific location. They are most likely to visit the resort and their unit regularly at the time of the week purchased.

Critical success factors largely concern relationships with staff at the resort and other resort owners. Social functions and opportunities to meet other guests are therefore also important critical success factors. Being recognized by resort staff and being treated as a valued customer, even a friend, by resort personnel are also critical to success.

These timeshare owners are less likely to swap their weeks or visits to another resort. They enjoy the familiarity, and like to get to know the place they are visiting. Sometimes, these timeshare owners will buy a timeshare property in areas which are of personal significance and are near the home origins of a parent, for example.

Swapper occasions

In direct contrast to the home from home occasion, some timeshare owners buy into a property never really intending to stay there. For them, the purchase is more akin to club membership that gives access to vacations in similar properties around the globe. Their property represents a currency through which they can purchase regular holidays with a greater sense of security.

Critical success factors include transparency and equivalence. All involved in the exchange process want to ensure that potential exchanges are clearly identified and that the process allows for consideration of the relative value of the week being given up by the owner and value of the property selected to exchange into.

The flexibility offered by these exchange systems has been a major factor in expanding the timeshare market because this opens up opportunities for more traditional tourist visits for those who do not want to be tied to a specific site every year. *Points Clubs*, whereby the consumer buys into a scheme, rather than a specific property allow this type of customer to have access to multiple destinations. Points clubs are natural and logical extensions of the 'swappers' need.

Activity occasions

Here the timeshare purchase is linked to some particular activity that is attractive to specific market segments. The activity might be associated with say golf, whereby customers want to have access to a good quality golf course.

Other activities might relate to walking holiday activities, cultural, or gaming/gambling and sporting activities say as in skiing or sailing or surfing activities.

Here the opportunity to use the course, or to have access to the specific features, such as walking, at times convenient to the owner, and at a reasonable charge are critical success factors.

Family holidays can be contradictory occasions because these may involve guests and service packages to guests that are not compatible with those who are interested chiefly in activity vacations.

Family holiday occasions

Timeshare purchase is concerned with providing a venue for family holidays. The week or weeks purchased are often consistent with school holidays, in some cases for the main holiday, in other cases, the timeshare purchase is associated with a second or third holiday. A timeshare property is one that contains attractions for the whole family.

Critical success factors relate to the extent that the property and the resort matches the needs of all the family members. Given the long-term nature of the timeshare relationship, it is likely that the venue will need to develop activities to match the various stages of the *Full-nest* outlined in Table 2.6.

This occasionality model is useful because it suggests that the reasons for purchasing a timeshare property vary, and that each decision to purchase involves some expectations of the benefits of the purchase and the factors critical to success. The occasionality model also suggests that motives and needs can vary, even for the same purchaser. Resort operators need to be aware of these changing needs.

Operators need to understand the impact on guest satisfaction of other guest occasions. *Complimentary occasions* occur when guests are sharing the same resort for different forms of occasionality, but this is compatible. Home from home customers and activity occasion guests might be an example, though the type of activity might be an issue. *Contradictory occasions* contradict this where different resort owners visit for occasions which conflict each other. This can happen between family holiday occasions and between activity occasion guests.

> **Key learning point 2.5**
> Occasionality suggests that timeshare owners may be buying timeshare properties for a cluster of different reasons which may cause clashes with other guests if reasons and motives are not compatible.

SUMMARY

This chapter attempts to provide some appreciation and tools to be able to understand both customers and their motives for buying into timeshare properties, and suggests how timeshare can be marketed effectively. In the best cases, timeshare brands have clearly defined qualities that are communicated to customers. In part, it is a managerial duty to ensure that customer expectations are at least met, if not exceeded when they stay in the resort. In these circumstances, understanding the nature of the service offer made by the brand and the critical factors needed for success are essential, because this gives work focus and objectives.

Further, the chapter has shown that those buying timeshare properties represent a quite tight range of potential customers. Individuals are largely drawn from the higher socio-economic groups; they are in an older age band and are in the later stages of a typical life cycle position. They are largely residents from the USA, UK and Germany with beaches being their most popular choices. That said, ownership spans many national and timeshare properties that can be found worldwide. Finally, timeshare ownership is often taken on for a narrow range of occasions some of which can be complimentary and others may be contradictory.

CHAPTER 3

The Community

After working through this chapter, you should be able to

- understand the fiscal impact of the timeshare industry
- discuss the different components that create the fiscal impact of the timeshare industry (sales, construction, operations, owner expenditures, and employment)
- identify the areas of spending that the timeshare industry most likely affects
- debate the legitimacy of timeshare development in a community

INTRODUCTION

The vacation ownership industry has clearly impacted the community where their resorts are housed. Because it is such a young industry comparable to the traditional lodging segment, there continues to be a pressing need to educate the public and local, state, and federal decision makers on the economic rewards that vacation ownership resorts bring to their communities.

This chapter will focus on recent economic indicators that show the pattern of positive gain in all areas related to tourism profit. This chapter will also give the reader a better understanding of vacation owners : their travel patterns and activities pursued while on vacation to get an overall picture of the type of visitor that is drawn to vacation ownership resorts.

CONTENTS

IMPACTS OF THE VACATION OWNERSHIP INDUSTRY

It is important to remember that the vacation ownership industry is multi-faceted. Similar to the lodging industry, the impacts are direct (the money for construction, the actual purchase of the product, employment at the actual resort, and taxes) and indirect (businesses needed to support the resort, employment opportunities created by the need, money spent at the businesses by vacation owners and guests, and the taxes on the money that is collected).

The impacts of the vacation ownership industry have been tracked from 2002 to 2005 (see Table 3.1). In every category, there has been an upward trend indicating a reliable positive impact based on the presence of vacation ownership resorts in a community.

The direct output impacts include jobs that were created by the need to build and employ the resort during the building/sales process and once construction is completed. The money spent at the resort by owners and guests is seen in the direct vacation expenditure impacts.

The indirect output impacts that result from the presence of vacation ownership resorts in a community are twofold: they include purchases by owners and guests in the community (e.g. money spent on souvenirs and at a grocery store) and they include employees and the income that is created by businesses needed to support the resorts (e.g. landscaping services and housekeeping contract services; see Table 3.2).

The final impact that communities benefit from as a result of vacation ownership resorts would be the taxes brought into the community (see Table 3.3).

Table 3.1	Direct Impacts of the Vacation Ownership Industry	
Direct impact	**2002**	**2005**
Direct output impacts	$17.2 billion of purchases	$22.6 billion of purchases
Direct resort impacts	102 900 jobs and $3.0 billion of salaries, wages, and related income	133 400 jobs and $4.5 billion of salaries, wages, and related income
Direct resort construction impacts	10 900 jobs and $490 million of salaries, wages, and related income	20 800 jobs and $960 million of salaries, wages, and related income
Direct vacation expenditure impacts	108 800 jobs and $2.6 billion of salaries, wages, and related income	99 700 jobs and $3 billion of salaries, wages, and related income
Total direct impact	$17.2 billion of output	$22.6 billion of output
	222 500 jobs	253 800 jobs
	$6.0 billion of income	$8.5 billion of income

Source: Price Waterhouse Cooper (2006) Economic impact of the timeshare industry on the US economy, ARDA International Foundation

Table 3.2	Indirect Impacts of the Vacation Ownership Industry	
Indirect Impact	**2002**	**2005**
Indirect output impacts	$27.1 billion of purchases	$39.2 billion of purchases
Indirect employment and income impacts	253 600 jobs, $10.2 billion of salaries, wages, and related income	311 500 jobs, $13.0 billion of wages, and related income
Total indirect impact	$27.1 billion of output 253 600 jobs $10.2 billion of income	$39.2 billion of output 311 500 jobs $13.0 billion of income

Source: Price Waterhouse Cooper (2006) Economic impact of the timeshare industry on the US Economy, ARDA International Foundation

Table 3.3	Fiscal Impacts of the Vacation Ownership Industry	
Fiscal Impact	**2002**	**2005**
Timeshare property and occupancy taxes	$380 million	$510 million
Timeshare employee taxes	$780 million	$968 million
Taxes on activities in other industries	$5.3 billion	$7.0 billion
Total fiscal input	$6.4 billion tax revenue	$8.5 billion tax revenue

Source: Price Waterhouse Cooper (2006) Economic impact of the timeshare industry on the US Economy, ARDA International Foundation

Based on the fact that these resorts are owned by those who live outside of the community, property taxes are collected for services such as schools that are never used by the owners. Also, it is still a rental property, and occupancy taxes are collected on the nightly rentals if the rooms are not being currently occupied by owners or exchangers. The employee taxes and taxes collected on activities pursued are both the positive result of an industry that sparks the economy by creating the need for employment and bringing in outside dollars to the community.

Key learning point 3.1

Timeshare resort operations contribute directly and indirectly to the local economy and contribute significantly to the tax base.

CASE STUDY

Donna Taylor is vice president of development of a timeshare company. She has found a wonderful location for the company's new timeshare resort development. It meets her company's needs of being the ideal location based on its proximity to popular attractions and restaurants. It also includes a large amount of acreage that she has been looking for in this destination.

She was quite thrilled to find the acreage for sale at a price that was well within the company's budget when she came up against the disapproval of the leaders of the community.

They do not want a timeshare resort located on the vacant acreage. Instead they want a signature hotel resort that can be the centrepiece of the destination. They believe that a hotel will attract more visitors and provide more jobs.

Now Donna has to convince the leaders of the community that the timeshare resort will be a worthwhile venture and it will provide just as many opportunities as a signature hotel resort. She now has to work on a presentation that will convince the community to be supportive of the timeshare resort development.

Reflective practice

[1] Read the case study and comment on why the community would prefer a signature hotel resort instead of a timeshare resort.

[2] What areas of impact will lend support to Donna's argument that a timeshare resort would be beneficial to the community?

[3] What would be the argument that would support what a timeshare resort could provide that a signature hotel resort could not?

[4] Timeshares have a less than favourable reputation in many circles. What could Donna present that would help quell their fears and biases?

TIMESHARE OWNER IMPACT AND VISITOR BEHAVIOUR

Economic impact has been broken down to more clearly understand how and where the money is being spent (see Table 3.4). The only category that has seen a decline between 2002 and 2005 is the spending per timeshare trip. However, this is looking at the entire timeshare resort, all guests including renters. Further down, the same question has been posed to timeshare owners, and this number has increased by 9.2% during the same time period. Another item of note is the average length of stay. In today's time of shorter vacations, the average length of stay continues to be longer than the traditional tourism market and continues to increase.

Every segment shows a pattern of increase from the size of the party to the number of extra nights spent in the resort area (see Table 3.5). During a time where the average tourist is more likely to take long weekend trips instead of

Table 3.4	Resort Statistics			
	2002	**2005**	**Change**	**Percent Change**
Number of timeshare units at year-end	132 000	154 439	22 439	17.0
Timeshare vacationers				
Number of timeshare trips (millions)	5.1	5.7	0.5	10.2
Average visitor party				
Number of people	3.6	3.8	0.2	6.1
Number of nights in resort area	7.6	8.1	0.5	5.9
Spending per timeshare trip	$1784	$1768	−$16	−0.9

Source: Price Waterhouse Cooper (2006) Economic impact of the timeshare industry on the US Economy, ARDA International Foundation

Table 3.5	Visitor Party Characteristics			
	2002	**2005**	**Change**	**Percent Change**
Number of people in visitor party				
Adults	2.9	3.0	0.1	3.5
Children (18 years and younger)	0.7	0.8	0.1	17.2
Total	3.6	3.8	0.2	6.1
Number of nights in resort area				
Timeshare resort (including timeshare bonus time or rental)	6.8	7.0	0.2	3.1
Other accommodations (including hotel, motel; RV; B&B; campsite, friends and family)	0.8	1.0	0.2	30.0
Total	7.6	8.1	0.5	5.9
Number of units occupied by visitor party				
Number of units (reflects the fact that a single travelling party may occupy more than one unit at a time)	1.1	1.2	0.0	4.4

Source: Price Waterhouse Cooper (2006) Economic impact of the timeshare industry on the US economy, ARDA International Foundation

week long trips, the timeshare guest proves to be a reliable tourist that is more likely to spend more money in the host community based on the size of the travelling party and the length of stay.

Interval International is one of the two largest vacation ownership exchange companies in the world (the other is Resort Condominiums International; see Chapter 8: The Role of Exchange Companies); its membership profile indicates the high level of income of the timeshare owner (see Table 3.6). Therefore, a rational assumption would be that the higher the

Table 3.6	Interval International Members Annual Income in 2006	
Total Household Income		**Percentage**
$74 999 and under		26.6
$75 000–$249 999		64.2
$250 000 and over		9.2
Mean		$139 800
Median		$108 200

Source: Simmons (2006) Interval International membership profile

income of the timeshare owner, the higher the discretionary income that the owner has to spend in the local community.

The Interval International member is also more likely to spend more than a week at a destination when their travel involves timeshare (see Table 3.7). They are also more likely to spend nights at hotel/motels. This is a group of people that take an active part in their travels. They are more likely to stay at their timeshare or hotel/motel than with friends or relatives. Based on their lodging preferences alone, the timeshare owner puts more money into the local economy that they visit.

Ragatz Associates (2006) determined that 90.5% of the available nights at timeshare resorts were used in some way by the owner (see Table 3.8). These results indicate a high occupancy rate in line with the occupancy rate of ARDA (2004), which reported the industry average of 85.6% for that year. This high occupancy is what makes timeshare such an ideal contributor to any community that wants to include tourism as part of their economic mix. The higher the occupancy, the greater the amount of money brought into the community by visitors. The greater need for year round employees reduces the seasonality which is the bane of existence of tourism's economy.

Table 3.7	Interval International Member Travel Behaviour – 2006		
Type of Accommodation	**Percentage of US Members Travelling for Leisure**	**Average Leisure Travel Nights**	**Average Length of Stay**
Hotel/motel	69.7	11.7	4.9
Timeshare	74.6	12.2	8.8
Other condo/vacation home	24.1	16.5	9.5
Villa/apartment	6.1	11.6	11.5
Friends/relatives	51.1	11.2	6.1
Other	3.2	17.0	10.2

Source: Simmons (2006) Interval International membership profile

Table 3.8	How Used was Timeshare(s) During the Past 12 Months (Average Percent of Available Nights)
Characteristic	**Percent of all Owners**
Used personally	35.8
Exchanged/space banked	47.4
Given away	2.9
Rented	4.4
Left unused (vacant)	9.5
Total	100

Source: Ragatz Associates (2006) Resort timeshare consumers: who they are, why they buy

The purchases of timeshares have skyrocketed (see Table 3.9). The number of weeks that are available have not kept pace, but this is based on the number of units sold in the preconstruction stage. The maintenance fees that are collected as well as the money by the timeshare company have increased and this makes sense due to inflation and the trend in timeshare resorts in providing a more luxurious experience for its owners and guests.

The upward pattern of the purchase price and maintenance fees paid coincide typically, because as the number of timeshare weeks owned increases, the amount of maintenance fees to be paid increases (see Table 3.10). Both have experienced double-digit increases reiterating the financial stability of the industry.

Ragatz Associates (2006) surveyed timeshare owners to get a better understanding as to specifically where they were spending their money while on vacation. In Table 3.11, these expenditures are given as per visitor party and not how much was spent per travelling group. The money is distributed

Table 3.9	Purchase and Maintenance Fee Impact				
		2002	**2005**	**Change**	**Percent Change**
Purchase of timeshares					
Purchases of timeshares (in millions, excludes resales)		$5500	$8600	$3112	56.6
Expenditures on maintenance fees					
Number of unit weeks available (in millions)		6.8	7.9	1.1	15.8
Average maintenance fee per unit week		$442	$496	$54	12.2
Total owner and timeshare company expenditures on maintenance fees (in millions)		$3010	$3910	$900	29.9

Source: Price Waterhouse Cooper (2006) Economic impact of the timeshare industry on the US economy, ARDA International Foundation

Table 3.10   Fiscal Impacts of Owner Purchases

Output Impact (In Millions)	2002	2005	Change	Percent Change
Direct purchases				
Purchases of timeshares	$5500	$8610	$3110	56.6
Expenditures on maintenance fees	$3010	$3910	$900	29.9
Owner expenditures during timeshare vacations	$9180	$10030	$850	9.2
Sub-total: direct purchases	$17690	$22550	$4860	27.5
Indirect purchases	$32210	$39,180	$6970	21.6
Total	$49900	$61730	$11830	23.7

Source: Price Waterhouse Cooper (2006) Economic impact of the timeshare industry on the US economy, ARDA International Foundation

Table 3.11   Expenditures While Vacationing in Resort Areas

Expenditures in Resort Area, all Owners (Per Visitor Party)	Per Vacation
Rental lodging, before or after staying in the timeshare unit	$85
Restaurant meals, take-away food, dinner shows, drinks in bars	$354
Groceries, sundries, liquor bought in stores	$136
Rental automobiles, gasoline, parking	$171
Sightseeing tours by bus, helicopter, boat, etc., and day cruises	$70
Other transportation such as buses and taxis	$18
Entertainment and sports activities (other than gaming, gambling)	$106
Net losses from gaming/gambling	$37
Shopping for items such as clothes, souvenirs, art, jewellery, handicrafts, etc. (other than food, sundries, or liquor)	$199
Admissions to attractions, movies, museums, rides, etc.	$110
Other expenses and services (not including any occupancy or maintenance fees charged by the timeshare resort)	$48
Total	$1334

Source: Ragatz Associates (2006). Resort timeshare consumers: who they are, why they buy

to many areas in a community with the highest amount going to restaurant meals, take-away food, dinner shows, drinks in bars and the lowest amount being spent on other transportation such as buses and taxis.

To get a better idea of the areas where the money is spent, Ragatz associates (2006) reports the expenditure per visitor party per day during timeshare vacations by type of resort areas (see Table 3.12). The gaming, gambling vacations receive the most money per visitor and the history, culture receive the least amount of money. It should be kept in mind that losses from gambling are included in this figure and that historic, cultural destinations tend to be less expensive than destinations that are in traditional resort areas.

Table 3.12	Average Expenditures Per Visitor Party Per Day During Timeshare Vacations by Type of Resort Area, all Owners
Activity	**Amount**
Gaming, gambling	$213
Tropics	$196
Snow skiing	$177
Desert	$177
City, urban	$160
Ocean beach	$160
Golf	$158
Mountains	$155
Attractions, entertainment	$153
Lake	$152
History, culture	$140

Source: Ragatz Associates (2006). Resort timeshare consumers: who they are, why they buy

Key learning point 3.2

Timeshare owners contribute to the local community through various ways: the purchase of timeshare, the annual maintenance fees paid, and the money spent while visiting the resort destination.

CASE STUDY

Donna Taylor has caught the attention of the community leaders based on the statistics that characterize the timeshare owner as affluent. There are other important attributes that she wants to make certain that they understand about the timeshare owner and how they can contribute to the economy of the community. She now realizes she must get back to work to ascertain whether the leaders see all the important contributions that the timeshare owner could bring to the community.

The other hurdle that she has is that the community wants to develop their historical and cultural attractions and one of the leaders pointed out that the timeshare owner actually spends less per day in these types of resorts than in any other type. They are concerned that even though the timeshare owner has money how can one be certain that they will spend it in their community.

Now Donna has her work cut out for her. She needs a plan to make sure that the leaders are convinced that the timeshare owner would make more contributions to their economy than tourists staying in a signature resort hotel. She also needs to quell their fears that they would be able to develop their historical and cultural attractions and still make money from a timeshare resort development instead of from a signature resort hotel.

EMPLOYMENT IMPACT OF THE TIMESHARE INDUSTRY

The employment impact of the timeshare industry has seen the largest increase in both the timeshare sales and marketing segment and resort construction (see Table 3.13). This would make sense because based on the increase in sales there is a need for more employees that would staff this area. The impact of resort operations is positive but does not keep pace with the other two because of the number of resorts that are in the preconstruction and construction stages.

The owner's expenditure while on timeshare trips has decreased. Interestingly enough the same figure in Table 3.12 shows an increase. The reason behind the discrepancy is that the figure in Table 3.12 indicates money that has been put in the community through expenditures, and the figure in Table 3.13 shows the jobs that were created and sustained based on the money that has been placed in the community through the owner's purchases on timeshare trips. This could be based on the fact that even though the spending amount goes up, the type of businesses where they are spending the money does not require as many employees. For example, the shift could be based on

Table 3.13 Employment Impact of the Timeshare Industry				
Employment Impact (Full-and Part-time Jobs)	**2002**	**2005**	**Change**	**Percent Change**
Direct employment				
Timeshare sales and marketing	27 700	42 100	15 100	55.8
Timeshare resort operations	84 000	91 300	7300	8.7
Resort construction	14 800	20 800	6000	40.8
Owner expenditures while on timeshare trips	108 900	99 700	−9300	−8.5
Sub-total: direct employment	234 700	253 800	19 100	8.2
Indirect employment	272 400	311 500	39 100	14.3
Total	507 100	565 300	58 200	11.5

Source: Price Waterhouse Cooper (2006) Economic impact of the timeshare industry on the US economy, ARDA International Foundation

a decrease in spending money in larger establishments such as theme parks and an increase in spending money at restaurants.

The impact of the employee salaries reflects the increase in employment. The sales and marketing segment has witnessed the most dramatic rise (see Table 3.14). However, the resort operations segment has seen a larger rise compared to the rise in jobs in the same segment as seen in Table 3.13. This indicates that the salary level of the employees had a more prominent increase than the rise in jobs which would mean higher wages for current employees in the timeshare industry. The resort construction saw a similar increase indicating that the employment opportunities in this area of the timeshare industry are garnering better financial gain.

It was mentioned in Table 3.13 that the timeshare owner's expenditures had resulted in a decline in employment that the money created from 2002 to 2005. The actual salaries that were supported as a result of this income increased slightly during the same period showing that although the timeshare owner's expenditures supported fewer jobs, the jobs the expenditures supported were for employment opportunities with higher wages. This lends support to the fact that the timeshare owners spend their money on experiences while visiting the community that are higher end (e.g., high end restaurants) than experiences that require more employees who earn less wages (e.g., theme parks).

The fiscal impact that the government relies on for its infrastructure and the sustainability of the tourism economy are the taxes collected from timeshare property and occupancy, employment taxes and taxes that have been generated from other industries as a result of timeshare resorts being part of the economy (see Table 3.15). As noted, employee salaries have increased, which directly results in an increase in taxes collected.

Table 3.14 Salary Impact of the Timeshare Industry				
Salaries, Wages, and Related Income Impact (In Millions)	2002	2005	Change	Percent Change
Direct employee compensation				
Timeshare sales and marketing	$1230	$2110	$880	71.2
Timeshare resort operations	$1770	$2380	$610	34.6
Direct labour income				
Resort construction	$640	$960	$320	50.0
Owner expenditures while on timeshare trips	$2990	$3040	$40	1.5
Sub-total: direct salaries, wages, and related Income	$6630	$8480	$1850	27.9
Indirect labour income	$10 620	$12 980	$2350	22.1
Total	$17 250	$21 460	$4200	24.4

Source: Price Waterhouse Cooper (2006) Economic impact of the timeshare industry on the US Economy, ARDA International Foundation

Fiscal Impact (In Millions)	2002	2005	Change	Percent Change
Table 3.15 Fiscal Impact of the Timeshare Industry				
Timeshare property and occupancy taxes	$430	$510	$80	18.4
Timeshare employee personal and social insurance taxes	$650	$970	$320	49.6
Taxes generated by activities in other industries	$5730	$7010	$1280	24.8
Total	$6800	$8480	$1680	24.8
Federal government tax impact	$3800	$4820	$1010	26.7
State and local government tax impact	$3000	$3670	$670	22.3

Source: Price Waterhouse Cooper (2006) Economic impact of the timeshare industry on the US economy, ARDA International Foundation

Key learning point 3.3

The employment impact of the timeshare industry is essential to the health of the community. It should be noted that the timeshare industry is known for the consistency of the income that is brought into the community. The design of the timeshare resort and how demand is handled results in less of an impact of seasonality.

CASE STUDY

Donna Taylor really won them over when she showed the community leaders the data concerning the economic impact of employment in the community as a result of timeshare resorts. They were thrilled to see such high numbers but they did voice some concerns.

One member was concerned that a large percentage was in sales and what would happen when timeshare resorts were sold out and the community was no longer benefiting from timeshare sales. Another member was concerned about the decrease in jobs that timeshare dollars had produced. They wanted to get a better understanding as to why there was a decrease in jobs from the timeshare dollars spent in the community but an increase in salaries as a result of the timeshare dollars in the community.

Donna now needs to assuage any fears that the leaders have and show them the ability of the timeshare resort to generate employment both inside and outside the gates of the resort. She needs to make sure that the leaders see every possible employment opportunity that is the result of the timeshare resort being in the community and why it would be a better choice to place a timeshare resort on a vacant piece of land and not in a signature hotel resort.

Reflective practice

[1] What kind of employment opportunities would be appropriate for sales professionals at a resort once the timeshare resort has been sold out? It is important to think long term and the community needs high income professionals to stay in the community for its long term health.

[2] What has led to the decline in the number of jobs that the timeshare owner's dollars support? If you were Donna Taylor, what would you tell the community leaders to quell any fears that they have about timeshare resort development?

[3] List out all the employment opportunities that exist in a community that would benefit from a timeshare resort development, both at the resort and in the community.

SUMMARY

The timeshare industry has a great deal to offer a host community in terms of stable employment opportunities and financial rewards. The timeshare owner provides a consistent stream of income into the community and research supports the addition of timeshare resorts as a favourable lodging development option. The knowledge of these positive impacts will help us to validate this segment of the industry and help developers be at a more agreeable vantage point when backed up by the potential host community, in future projects.

CHAPTER 4

Marketing Vacation Ownership Resorts

After working through this chapter, you should be able to

- define what marketing is

- recognize what components fall under the marketing umbrella

- identify the types of marketing that the vacation ownership industry has traditionally employed

- identify the types of marketing that the vacation ownership industry needs to employ to effectively compete in a changing marketplace

INTRODUCTION

There has traditionally been a wide discrepancy between the marketing methods that vacation ownership resorts routinely employ and the marketing methods that other products routinely employ. Because of this, it is imperative to understand what constitutes marketing, the difference between inbound and outbound marketing and what components fall under the broad marketing umbrella before we look at the ways in which the vacation ownership product is marketed.

This chapter outlines the components of the marketing mix which are said to differentiate between manufactured goods and services. It is interesting to ponder whether timeshare is a product or a service. Clearly, the unit – villa or apartment – is a product based on the purchase of tangible assets. On the other hand, the vacation aspect of the purchase represents a cluster of intangible services. But then, many purchases in both products and services are in reality a combination of both tangible and intangible benefits to the consumer.

CONTENTS

THE MARKETING MIX

The marketing mix is a way of thinking about goods and services supplied. Initially, products were said to involve four key components – product, price, place, promotion – and these could be manipulated by marketers to differentiate one offer to customers from another. Subsequently, it was felt that marketing of services needed another set of components so as to take more account of the intangible elements of the service encounter. The following seven components represent the service marketing mix.

Product: The product aspects of marketing deal with the specifications of the actual good or service, and how it relates to the end-user's needs and wants. The scope of a product generally includes supporting elements such as warranties, guarantees and support.

Pricing: This refers to the process of setting a price for the product.

Promotion: This includes advertising, sales promotion, publicity and personal selling.

Placement: This is also known as distribution and refers to how the product gets to the client.

When marketers deal with a service rather than with a product, they routinely rely on additional '3 Ps'.

People: Any person coming into contact with clients has an impact on overall satisfaction or dissatisfaction. People are important because, in the client's mind, they are inseparable from the total service.

Process: This tells us how the service is provided and the behaviour of the people involved, which is critical to customer satisfaction.

Physical evidence: Unlike a product, a service is intangible and cannot be experienced before use. Services generally have more risk associated with them in a client's minds. Physical evidence can be provided through the use of testimonials or case studies

CASE STUDY

Referring back to the '7Ps'-Product, Pricing, Promotion, Placement, People, Process and Physical Evidence - answer the following questions:

MARKETING TIMESHARE

Inbound marketing

Inbound Marketing is another term for Market Research. The point in conducting market research is to determine the following:

- What specific groups known as 'target markets' of clients have specific needs

- How the product could meet those needs

- How the clients can access the product

- How much the clients would be willing to pay

- Whether the product has any competition, and who the competitor is

- How the product is designed and described so that the target markets will choose to purchase that product and not the competitor's

- What the product's story, brand and/or identity is

Outbound marketing

Outbound marketing is made up of what is known as traditional advertising, that is getting the message, the offer and the product out to the client. Outbound Marketing includes:

- advertising and promotions

- sales

- public and media relations

- customer service

- customer satisfaction

> **Key learning point 4.1**
> It is imperative that vacation ownership resorts conduct the Inbound Marketing process before beginning the Outgoing Marketing process. If they don't, they will end up trying to sell their product to people who really don't want the product at all.

Now that we have a brief understanding of what the purpose of marketing is, and what it constitutes, we can look at how the vacation ownership industry has routinely marketed itself.

1980 snapshot

The phone rings at Mr and Mrs Smith's home. The caller says, 'Congratulations Mr and Mrs Smith! You've won a free television. Do you have a pen and a piece of paper? All you have to do is come to (ADDRESS) on (DATE) between the hours of 10:00 am and 2:00 pm to claim your prize. We look forward to seeing you!'

Mr and Mrs Smith do in fact show up at the appointed place on the appointed date and are herded into a large conference room with 100 or so other 'lucky' winners and are subjected to a 2 hour and 45 minute long timeshare sales presentation.

After politely saying 'NO' five or six times to five or six different salespersons and managers, each more high pressure than the last, Mr and Mrs Smith are finally brought to a tiny room to claim their prize – a 7″ black and white TV. The retail value of the prize? About $50.00.

Although Mr and Mrs Smith did not make any purchase, about 10% of the other clients, all of whom were there because they 'won' a free television, did make a purchase.

2008 snapshot

The phone rings at Mr and Mrs Smith's home. The caller says, 'Congratulations Mr and Mrs Smith, you've qualified for a free Orlando vacation. Yes, 3 days and 2 nights in sunny Orlando, Florida. And because you qualify, we're also going to give you 2 tickets to a theme park of your choice. All of this for only $199 to cover taxes. This is a limited time offer so press 1 to book now before your date is gone.'

Mr and Mrs Smith receive their packet of information by mail a few days later and make their arrangements to visit Orlando.

Four months later, an exhausted Mr and Mrs Smith arrive after a 4 hour drive at a run-down hotel that looks nothing like the beautiful pictures in the material. Before they get their room keys, they are told that they have to attend a 'presentation' the next morning at 8:00 at another location.

Bleary-eyed, Mr and Mrs Smith show up the next morning and are greeted by a well-dressed young man who allows them to eat a bagel and drink some coffee before starting a 2 hour and 45 minute sales presentation.

Mr. and Mrs. Smith politely say no about five or six times to two or three people, each having a 'better offer' than the last and finally leave more aggravated than when they walked in.

Although Mr and Mrs Smith did not make any purchase, about 10% of the other clients, all of whom were there because they 'qualified' for the free vacation, did make a purchase.

Notice any similarities?

- In 1980, about 10% of the clients made a purchase.

- In 2008, about 10% of the clients made a purchase.

- In 1980, no mention was made of a timeshare presentation prior to the clients showing up.

- In 2008, no mention was made of a timeshare presentation prior to the clients showing up with the exception of some very fine print on the printed materials that were sent to the client.

- In 1980, the client received no information about the timeshare product or concept.

- In 2008, the client received no information about the timeshare product or concept.

Notice any differences?

- In 1980, the cost to bring Mr and Mrs Smith into the selling room was about $100.

- In 2008, the cost to bring Mr and Mrs Smith into the selling room was about $375.

- In 1980, Mr and Mrs Smith had never heard about timeshare, nor had they been on a timeshare sales presentation.

- In 2008, Mr and Mrs Smith know 'how to work the system'…this is their third timeshare presentation in 18 months and the first of two they have scheduled for that day.

As you can see, timeshare marketing has changed very little from how it was in 1980. So why is an obviously flawed system still in place?

First of all, timeshare generates nearly $10 billion annually. But if you speak with anyone who has a marketing background outside of timeshare, they are quick to realize that it could be a much larger number. The fact is that after 35 years, **less than 5% of the population owns timeshare.** In other businesses, less than 5% market penetration would not be thought sufficient, considering that **more than 5% of the population spends money on vacations.**

To understand these skewed numbers, let us take a closer look at the ways in which timeshare is marketed, review the main reasons why clients do not purchase the product, offer some suggestions for improving the system and look ahead to a possible scenario in 2018.

VACATION OWNERSHIP MARKETING PRACTICES

There are several different marketing practices that timeshare resorts use to market their resort to potential owners. They include the following:

- Off property consultant
- Drawing drop boxes
- Telemarketing
- Mini-vacations (mini-vacs)
- Internet
- Direct mail
- Print advertisements
- Television advertisements
- Billboards

The next section will discuss the current marketing techniques.

Off property consultant (OPC)

OPCs are ubiquitous in locations such as Orlando, Las Vegas, Cancun, and other vacation destinations. OPCs may be located in a hotel lobby, a roadside tourist information booth, a casino floor, outside a restaurant, in a theme park, in a shopping mall, etc. The purpose is to find a high traffic tourist location. They offer discounted tickets to attractions, discounted meals at local restaurants, and other relevant enticements to get a commitment to go on a timeshare tour. The rent for leasing the OPC space can be as low as zero dollars if it is on the resort property or as high as $10 000 a month for a valued location such as a casino floor in Las Vegas.

Those employed at OPCs usually work on commission basis, so training and monitoring need to be in place to ensure that they are maintaining the company's standards. This is vital because in many cases it is the first impression a person has in mind about the resort. Also, a reward system needs to be in place to ensure that quality tours are booked. This means that people understand that they are going on a tour of a resort, that they meet the minimum age requirement, if any, that they have the minimum income required, that both parties are present in the case of a married couple, and that they meet any other requirement that the resort has. A side note is that most resorts require that both spouses attend the tour to receive any incentive (e.g., discounted tickets) for going on the tour. The reason is that it is not likely that someone will make such a decision on such an important purchase alone.

When persons qualify for a tour (based on their age, income, presence of spouse (if applicable), they will be invited to go on a tour. An appointment is made and usually a refundable deposit (around $20) is collected to make certain that they will show up for the tour.

Drawing drop boxes

Drawing drop boxes are those that are housed in stores or in restaurants that offer a drawing for a free prize or a way for people to submit their names to see whether they qualify for a discounted vacation. The form that they fill out includes their mailing address, e-mail address, and phone number, so the resort must follow up with telemarketing, e-mail, or direct mail. The forms must also include the fact that this opportunity will include a timeshare presentation.

Telemarketing

The 'Do Not Call' legislation was passed in around 2003, and it has caused the industry to focus on other means of marketing, although telemarketing is still in place in the timeshare industry. People that are not part of the 'Do Not Call' list, members of loyalty programs at brand companies, people that fill out information in drawing drop boxes, and people that request information on the Internet are all included in the focus of telemarketing efforts.

Telemarketing efforts are used to invite guests to the resort area for a mini-vacation often known as 'mini-vac'(three days, two nights sometimes shorter or longer in length). The mini-vac is offered at a discounted rate, and in return, the guest must attend a timeshare presentation, failing which they will be charged the regular rack rate for the room night. The min-vac has a better closing rate because people plan for the timeshare tour to be included in their vacation plans, ahead of time.

Some companies use rapid dialers with computerized voices that announce the opportunity to the person at the other end, but a more personalized experience is more likely to produce results for the resort. A well-trained representative clearly states the purpose of the call and why they should include a trip to a vacation destination where they would go on a timeshare tour as a part of their vacation plans.

In the same vein as employees that work at OPC locations it is imperative that they are well trained. Again, this could be the person's first impression of the resort, and people tend to be disinclined to listen to a telemarketer, so they must be skilled in getting someone's attention in a pleasant manner in a short period of time. Telemarketers are also paid on commission basis, so monitoring their calls is essential. This makes it certain that they are being truthful and appealing in what they are offering and makes it certain whether the persons understand that they must go on a timeshare tour to qualify for the discounted lodging rate.

Internet

The Internet has become a popular marketing medium. As more and more people use the Internet daily, timeshare resorts have used the Internet to introduce people to their product through virtual tours of their resorts and descriptions of the product's benefits. People are also invited to enter their contact information so that they can be sent additional information about the product, and for those who qualify a telemarketer will most likely follow up with an invitation for a mini-vac.

Direct mail

Many resorts send out postcards or another form of direct mail informing clients that they have won, or in some way have qualified to receive a discounted vacation, that is 'mini-vac' of some sort. This type of mailing needs to be eye-catching because of the abundance of junk mail people often receive and a great deal of money going into the product.

Some of these offers are quite elaborate – mass produced invitations on 'certificate' paper, complete with official looking stamped numbers and a myriad of 'extra bonuses' such as cruises and dinner show tickets if the client calls within a certain time frame. The invitations help minimise the problems involved in 'Do Not Call' restrictions because clients tend to call the telemarketer themselves. Also, persons can call when it is convenient for them instead of getting interrupted by a telemarketer.

Again, in most jurisdictions, the disclaimer requires the 'reason' for the offer. The language of the disclaimer, or the legal purpose of the offer, varies from jurisdiction to jurisdiction, but is similar to 'This advertising material is being used for the purpose of soliciting the sales of timeshare periods.'

Print advertisements

Advertisements in the travel section of newspapers and even some magazines have been a marketing medium that does have some appeal because it contains a picturesque view of the resort or the resort's environs with an invitation to contact a certain telephone number or a web address to find out about the mini-vac that is offered in the advertisement. There is a notification that a tour of the resort is mandatory to qualify for the special offer. High-end fractionals have been advertising in some of the magazines that market to a more exclusive market base as well.

Television advertisements

Because television advertising is so expensive and it is hard to explain a timeshare resort and its benefits in a 30 second commercial, it is being used very sparingly. It is used to peak someone's interest where at the end they are directed to a web site. As this product grows in acceptability and the public becomes more educated about the product, chances are that television advertisements will increase.

Billboard advertisements

Billboards are sometimes located on busy thoroughfares where timeshare resorts are located. However, similar to television advertisements, they only act as a teaser, and because so much money is spent in other marketing areas, this is rarely used as a marketing medium.

Key learning point 4.2

Marketing in the timeshare industry is multi-faceted; however, the primary goal is the timeshare tour. In the future, as product costs continue to rise, cuts in marketing costs will be essential. Targeting the consumer that is most likely to buy the timeshare needs to be the primary focus during the next decade so that money can be saved. People with no interest or qualifications to purchase timeshares should not be invited on tours while more focused forms of marketing need to be increased.

CASE STUDY

Jean is trying to choose a marketing plan for his resort. Rooms at the resort are rented out for $109 per night in the off-season. He has to choose between the ones that James and Jessica are proposing.

James proposes purchasing a phone list and cold-calling consumers, with an offer of three days and two nights at the resort and two dinner show tickets for $149 with the stipulation that the client attend the required sales presentation.

Jessica proposes offering the same three-day and two-night stay for $150 with no dinner show tickets included, but offering instead an 'instant rebate' of $100 if the client chooses to purchase a timeshare during the required sales presentation.

Reflective practice

1. Do you think Jean should choose James' or Jessica's plan and why?
2. Would you change anything in either of the offers?
3. Discuss how resorts have the ability to target their prospects and ultimately, customize their owner base.
4. Is this a good idea? Yes or No and why?

Relationship marketing

Relationship marketing refers to the practice of getting to know the customer and finding out their likes and dislikes about the product. It continues over the lifetime the resort has contact with the customer and is dependent on the trust the customer has for the resort. The following methods are referred to as relationship marketing practices because they use positive word of mouth, follow-up marketing attempts, and trial memberships to build the relationship between the resort and customer.

Referrals

Most timeshare resorts have some sort of a referral program in place. Referral programs typically reward existing owners for referring clients in the hope that the client will also make a purchase.

There are several benefits for instituting and maintaining a good referral program. These are as follows:

- lower marketing costs for the resort
- a feeling of 'belonging' for the initial client

- less fear and trepidation on the part of the referred client

- the referred client (and the salesperson) know from the outset that there is a valid reason to attend the sales presentation, that is the client has not been brought to the resort as a result of some other marketing practice

Some resorts reward clients with cash, others with points or other credit to be used only at the resort. Some referral programs reward the client for any referral that comes to the resort and attends the sales presentation, regardless of whether they make a purchase or not.

The following is an example of a resort's referral program:

OWNER REFERRAL PROGRAMS

Our Owner Referral Program is SIMPLE! It's a great way to earn cash that you can apply towards your maintenance and taxes, mortgage or to spend however you please! It's our way of saying 'THANK YOU' for being an owner with us.

You will be awarded $50 for every qualified referral that takes advantage of our VIP vacation package and attends a 90-minute tour and sales presentation at NAME OF RESORT.

If one of your referrals chooses to experience high quality vacations for a lifetime, just as you did, we also reward you with $500.00 for their annual vacation interval purchase or $250.00 for a bi-annual vacation interval purchase.

Refer your friends and family and we'll do the rest. Just think of who you know that would appreciate the way that you're already accustomed to vacationing.

When you refer your friends and family to us, they get to enjoy a fabulous vacation at a discounted rate:

- Your referrals will be invited to stay with us on property in a 1-bedroom villa for 4 days and 3 nights.

- Their package will also include a choice of two attraction tickets or $75 for dinner for two.

The whole package is only **$249.00** (plus tax).

We can start today! If you have the names and numbers of people that you feel would enjoy a vacation here at RESORT, we'll be happy to contact them immediately. We'll also give you everything you need to refer people once you leave the resort.

Referral programs are generally required to be registered with the jurisdiction that the resort's home base is in and based on the jurisdiction, there are rules as to what an owner can receive for giving the resort a referral.

Tour no-buys

Another way that resorts routinely keep the tour numbers up is to solicit the same clients that have previously toured the resort and not purchased. Although at first glance, this may seem like a waste of marketing dollars, clients are again enticed with a discounted stay and/or other sometimes-costly incentives, tour no-buys may be worthwhile to the resort particularly when we understand the reasons why consumers do not make any purchase.

Trial programmes

Trial programmes are sometimes offered to those on tours who do not want to buy that day but are interested in the product. The trial program can include one week at the timeshare for the coming year and if they decide to buy the timeshare during the trial period, they can apply the cost of the trial membership to the cost of the timeshare.

Why consumers don't buy

The 2006 Study by Ragatz and Associates entitled 'A Survey of Non-Buyers of Resort Timeshare' gives the reasons for consumers not purchasing (Table 4.1).

Given that almost 70% of the respondents cited the issue of purchasing on the same day of the sales presentation as a 'very important' reason for not

CASE STUDY

The Marketing Manager at Acme Resort plans to implement two separate programs to determine which one is more effective and more successful for the resort.

In the first plan, clients who did not purchase at the resort are contacted by means of a phone call within six months of their initial sales presentation and given the opportunity to stay at the resort for three days and two nights for a discounted price of only $159.

In the second plan, the client is also contacted with a similar option, but this time, the invitation is sent as a letter,

personally signed by the salesperson and has numerous references to questions and concerns that the client initially voiced, such as 'By the way, I know that you had expressed interest in how high the annual dues may go, I'd like to let you know that we only had a 1.2% increase this year,' or 'I'm sending you a reprint of a recent article in the Wall Street Journal that mentioned how much the typical consumer benefits from owing timeshare.'

purchasing; it makes sense to give those consumers another opportunity to purchase.

It is interesting to note how many timeshare sales presentations are attended by consumers. Elsewhere in the Ragatz report referred to earlier, these data are given (see Table 4.2).

These results are confirmed when coupled with the findings of the 2006 Ragatz Associates report 'Resort Timeshare Consumers: Who They Are,

Table 4.1 Declared Reasons for Non-Purchases		
Reason for not Purchasing	**% Very or Somewhat Important**	**% Very Important**
Do not make same-day purchase decisions for such expensive items	89	69.5
Price was too high	84.3	54.3
Prefer to be more flexible with my choice of vacation	80	51.2
Annual maintenance fees were too high	77.0	41.7
Not sure we would make enough use of it	73.7	42.1
Monthly payments were too high	70.0	38.4
Did not seem like a good value	67.8	31.6
Down payment was too high	65.5	33.9
Travel to resort too expensive or inconvenient	64.2	27.7
Sales presentation was too high pressure	63.6	33.7
Wondered if it was 'too good to be true'	62.6	30.8
Attended only to receive the gift or min-vacation (never interested in purchasing)	59.1	23.0
Exchange option with other resorts was not clear	57.1	23.2
Had heard, read or experienced something negative about resort timesharing	51.5	23.8
Did not think there were enough or the right kind of activities and amenities	50.2	15.9
Personality or appearance of the salesperson	44.6	18.6
Did not like the geographic location of the salesperson	41.5	13.3
Did not care for the resort itself	39.0	12.9
Advised against it by friend, relative, attorney, etc.	32.5	10.6
Did not like method of invitation to attend sales presentation	32.4	9.8

Table 4.2	The Number of Timeshare Presentations Attended by Age Groups		
	Under Age 45	**Age 45–54**	**Over Age 55**
Total previous sales presentations attended			
0	39.4	20.2	13.9
1	11.0	8.4	5.8
2	20.4	22.5	16.4
3	29.3	48.9	63.8
Mean	1.8	3.2	4.6

Why They Buy,' which reported that in 2005, the average timeshare buyer has attended 2.6 sales presentations before making their purchase referred to in the study.

Why consumers buy

According to the same Ragatz report, the motivations rated as 'very important' to buyers in 2005 are given in Table 4.3.

It is interesting to note that the 'same day purchase incentive' that nearly all timeshare resorts offer, which will be discussed further in Chapter 5 on Sales, was a very important factor to only 40.7% of the respondents.

Considering the information about why people purchase, why they don't purchase, the fact that consumers typically attend 2.6 timeshare

Table 4.3	Declared Reasons for Making a Purchase
Attribute	**% Rated as Very Important**
Overall flexibility	89.4
Certainty of quality accommodations	81.7
Credibility of timeshare company	75
Internal exchange	74.9
External exchange	72.6
Location of resort	69.2
Liking for resort, amenities, unit	68.2
Saving money on future vacations	65.9
Opportunity to own at an affordable price	56.6
Treatment during sales presentation	56.2
Affordable financial terms	53.2
Method, politeness of sales invitation	45.1
Same day purchase incentive	40.7

presentations before making a purchase and the fact that only 40.7% of buyers found the first visit incentive or discount important, we can be reasonably certain that consumers prefer to comparison shopping for timeshare products rather than buying the timeshare when they have not had enough time to educate themselves about their purchase.

> **Key learning point 4.3**
>
> Timeshare consumers, as most other consumers, prefer to buy products and/or services as opposed to being sold those same products and/or services. Timeshare resorts have historically operated in a manner which goes against this underlying preference.

2018 snapshot

Mr and Mrs Smith from Princeton, West Virginia, have previously attended three timeshare sales presentations while on vacation in Cancun, Mexico; Daytona Beach, Florida; and Myrtle Beach, South Carolina. While planning their next vacation to Las Vegas, Nevada, they decide to go to the brand new Timeshare Shop in Mercer Mall, just 15 minutes from home.

Shawn, the Customer Service Representative, asks Mr and Mrs Smith some questions about their vacation likes and dislikes, their annual vacation expenditures and what they are looking for in a timeshare product.

Based on their answers, Shawn gives Mr and Mrs Smith a list of three timeshares that fit their needs. Each of the timeshares has a clearly defined price listed, and there are no 'first visit' incentives applicable, but the prices are valid for the next 30 days.

The Smiths return home and some days later, go over the list of timeshare resorts. One week later, they call Shawn and tell him that they would like to purchase the point-based timeshare resort in San Antonio, Texas.

SUMMARY

Timeshare marketing relies more on outbound marketing, while putting less emphasis on inbound marketing. It has been demonstrated that overall marketing functions play a large role in why consumers do not purchase timeshare. Placing the emphasis on the product, rather than on an incentive of some kind and giving consumers more time to make an educated choice may result in better consumer attitudes and higher sales efficiencies in the future.

CHAPTER 5

The 12-Step Sales Process: Part 1

'People buy with emotion and justify it with logic.'

After working through this chapter, you should be able to

- identify the 12 steps of the sales process

- understand the importance of making certain that clients are at ease with the intent statement

- understand why the discovery is key to a good sales process

- clearly differentiate between first-, second- and third-level questions

INTRODUCTION

The sales process in the timeshare industry is obviously essential for the project's success. It takes a refined process to explain the product briefly and receive a commitment to purchase the product that costs a significant amount of money. Although a majority of clients report that they did not attend the presentation with an intention to purchase, statistics reveal that approximately one out of every 10 of them do. This chapter will illustrate to the reader the important role that the timeshare salesperson plays in the sales process and how asking the right questions, timing and, most importantly, listening are key to a successful sales presentation.

CONTENTS

THE 12-STEP SALES PROCESS

Although different resorts sometimes condense this sales process into as few as five or ten steps, there are 12 distinct steps that the salesperson must accomplish to have a chance at a sale. These steps are given in Table 5.1.

Preparation

Both the client and the timeshare staff must be adequately prepared. The timeshare staff, including but not limited to front desk personnel, salespersons and sales managers, must be mentally and physically prepared. The clients must also be mentally prepared. Since almost all of the clients arriving at the timeshare resort will be there because they are fulfilling some sort of obligation to get something (discounted vacation, dinner certificate, etc.), it is imperative for them to understand that they will be attending a sales presentation.

It is important for salespeople as well as everyone who has contact with customers to remember that the tone of everyone's day starts with attitude.

A few words about attitude are as follows:

- We all choose our attitude; it is not the result of external forces. Although it is true that salespeople cannot choose what happens to them, whom they meet, how much money those people have, etc., we can and should always be aware that we can choose our response to those people and those situations.

- It is quite common in timeshare sales that the salespeople with the worst attitude try to recruit others to their ranks. A smart salesperson

Table 5.1	Twelve Steps of the Sales Process
Step One	Preparation
Step Two	Greeting
Step Three	Intent statement
Step Four	Warm-up
Step Five	Discovery
Step Six	Information confirmation
Step Seven	Presentation or uncovering of problem
Step Eight	Product features
Step Nine	Property viewing
Step Ten	Solution of problem
Step Eleven	Closing
Step Twelve	Follow-up

should seek out salespeople and managers with good attitudes. Attitude is highly contagious.

■ No salesperson, however prepared, however positive and/or however educated will sell every single client. Rather than dwelling on a sale that was not made, smart salespersons will seek out what they can learn from that encounter, and will put the actual sales experience behind them. Do not dwell on past experiences, good or bad. Every single encounter with a client is a learning experience.

Physical preparation for the timeshare staff manifests itself not only in basic grooming and wearing a proper business attire, but also in an understanding of what makes for a comfortable environment for all concerned.

> **Key learning point 5.1**
> A positive mental attitude is crucial for salespeople. Every experience, regardless of whether it results in a sale or not, should be considered a learning experience.

Greeting

First impressions count for everything. When the salesperson meets his or her clients for the first time, both the client and the salesperson immediately make judgements about the other. Within the first 60 seconds of meeting, the clients make judgements based on the salesperson's stance, vocal inflections, dress, breath and other physical characteristics. The salesperson also makes immediate judgements based on the same criteria. Pre-judging clients to determine whether they will or will not buy is deadly and is the sign of a weak salesperson. However, the client will pre-judge, and this will affect the way they feel about the salesperson during the entire sales presentation, good or bad.

The salesperson needs to be direct, friendly, self-assured and should appear to be interested right off the bat. Although many timeshare resort salespersons insist on giving the client a firm handshake at the initial meeting, many clients find this an invasion of their personal space at this early stage.

It is important to note that at this early stage, many salespeople know next to nothing about their client and vice versa. Most resorts give the salesperson nothing more than just a slip of paper with the client's name on it, or perhaps the clients' name is written on a series of papers that the discovery will be used for. As mentioned before, first impressions can lead to serious business. The front desk personnel should clearly write the client's name to minimize any chances the salesperson has to mispronounce the client's name.

The salesperson will generally come out to a reception area where many clients are waiting. It is important to be quick, direct, friendly and clear. 'Good Morning, Mr. and Mrs. Smith...' or 'Good Morning, I'm looking for the Smith family...' are two good ways of greeting clients.

On meeting the client, salespersons should immediately introduce themselves and lead the clients into the area where the sales presentation will be taking place. Depending on what the physical layout of the sales room is, the salesperson should lead the clients to his or her area, which may be nothing more than just a small table.

Intent statement

Sometimes called the order of the day, the intent statement is a simple, oftentimes missed, and yet a crucial step. The client may or may not have been on a prior sales presentation. It is too early to ask. It is however vitally important to tell the client exactly what will be happening while they are there. The best intent statements combine verbal and written information and conclude with a positive confirmation given to the salesperson from the client.

Why is an intent statement crucial? Timeshare non-buyers cite '"lack of trust' as one of the main reasons for not making a purchase. Trust or lack thereof starts with the intent statement given by the salesperson. The salesperson must be careful to follow through on every aspect of their intent statement. Therefore, if the salesperson's intent statement contains something about seeing the property, it is imperative that the client sees the property. Oftentimes, the client will receive a gift of some sort after the presentation, and it is this gift that they are most focused on at this early stage. The salesperson needs to reassure clients that they will indeed receive this gift regardless of whether a purchase is made or not.

The importance of letting the client know that the salesperson will be asking them to purchase at the end of the presentation cannot be too strongly stressed. Good intent statements (example given later) use the word 'TODAY' several times. Good salespersons use the word 'TODAY' several times throughout the presentation.

The facts are simple: Virtually none of the clients attending timeshare sales presentations come with the intent to purchase. This text has already addressed the marketing issues facing the industry today and the fact that the public will be forcing a change. Yet, the vast majority of the $9 billion timeshare sales are done 'TODAY.'

Letting clients know that they will be asked to make a decision or more likely a choice about purchasing today must be clear and must be repeated. Because less than 10% of communication is verbal, using the word 'TODAY'

Table 5.2	Intent Statement

Timeshare today is as easy as 5, 4, 3, 2, 1

There are five parts of today's presentation…first, I'll be asking you some questions about your vacations; secondly we'll talk a little about money – what you spend on your vacations and what it gets you; thirdly, I'll tell you a little about our timeshare; fourth and more important, we'll discover how it can make your vacations better and of course, you'll get a chance to see the resort for yourself

There are four words that are very important here today. Those words are Value, Flexibility, Courage and Commitment

We'll be answering three questions today. Why do you go on vacation? What about timeshare works for you? Why should you purchase today?

You have two choices available to you today. You can choose YES or you can choose YES. What that means is that you can say yes you like it, yes you would use it and yes you want to buy it, or you can choose to say yes you like it, yes you would use it and yes you are going to continue to vacation your way.

So that leaves one outcome from whichever yes you choose today. Your choice will impact you much more than it will impact me. What that means is that I will not play games with you and I will not pressure you to buy anything today.

and demonstrating to the client that they do indeed make choices and decisions all the time without having to think about it are tools that the successful salesperson will use.

One of the best and most clear-cut intent statements is given in Table 5.2.

Intent statements should always end with the salesperson asking all the clients, 'Is that OK with you?' and offering and receiving a handshake and giving a sincere 'Thank You.' This is a good time to address male vs. female difference. Male salespersons should address the male client first and then the female client. Female salespersons should do the opposite. If a male salesperson addresses the female client first, both clients will oftentimes interpret this as a sign of aggressiveness and vice versa with female salespersons.

CASE STUDY

Janet, a salesperson with seven years of experience, met her clients one morning for a sales presentation. She introduced herself, offered her clients breakfast and spent 15 minutes chit-chatting.

After breakfast, Janet started asking her clients some questions about vacations, told them about the many features the resort offered and found out that the clients had spent a sleepless night at a nearby motel due to the noise by the pool area.

The clients seemed to like the resort very much and commented that they wished they were staying on-premise rather than at their motel. Janet seemed pleased and as they were walking back to the sales centre thought that she had a sale.

Janet showed the clients the price of the one-bedroom that they had liked so much and asked them to purchase it. The clients looked surprised, and one of them said to Janet, 'We didn't know this was a sales pitch, we just wanted to see this so we could stay here next time we go on vacation.'

Reflective practice

1. Read the case study and comment on why an intent statement is imperative.

2. Besides delivering a concise intent statement, what else could Janet have done to improve her chances of a sale?

3. What practices could resort management put into place to reduce the chances of this happening again?

Key learning point 5.2

An intent statement, also known as an 'order of the day' serves a key purpose for both the client and the salesperson. It lets the client know exactly what is going to happen and it keeps the salesperson on track.

Warm-up

No client, however logical, will ever purchase anything from a salesperson who is cold, unfriendly and above all uninterested. A warm-up or getting to know the client step is therefore imperative. However, it should be stated that too many salespersons make the error of doing too much of a warm-up which has the ultimate effect of making it easier for the client to say 'no' at the end. A terse introduction is too short and a 45-minute 'touchy-feely' sharing conversation is too long.

What is a warm-up designed to do and how long should it last?

A warm-up is simply designed for the salesperson to get to know the client as something other than a client, and for the client to get to know the salesperson as something other than a salesperson. Individual styles vary of course, but a good warm-up should last between 10 and 15 minutes, based on a typical 90–120 minute complete sales presentation.

A warm-up is NOT the time to discuss timeshare, or even vacation. A good rule of thumb for the salesperson is to concentrate on FOR – family, occupation and recreation. People like to talk about themselves, so a salesperson should ask the client about himself or herself and possibly share some information about them, particularly if asked or when there is a chance to establish some commonality.

Questions related to FOR – family, occupation and recreation – can and oftentimes do uncover dominant buying motives, which will be discussed in the section on Discovery.

Table 5.3	Warm-up Questions

Examples of Warm-up Questions:

Where are you from?
Have you lived there your whole life?
What is the best thing about that place?
What do you do for a living?
How long have you been doing it?
What do you like best about your job?
How many children do you have?
Do the children have any after school activities or sports?
What is your favourite hobby?
Did you receive any special training for your job?
What are you most looking forward to doing when you retire?
What are your children's names?
Is this your first visit to (this place)?
What do you like to do for entertainment back home?

The warm-up is often done as the client and salesperson are eating together. Breakfast or lunch, as part of the resort's offering, can range from donuts and coffee to a full buffet lunch and will be looked at more closely in the section on Sales Environment. The salesperson should take care not to take notes during this part of the process. However, the salesperson must take care to remember what is being discussed and what the client says. Although it sounds calculating, one must never forget that everything that happens during the short 90–120 minute presentation should take both parties one step closer to a sale (Table 5.3).

Discovery

The discovery is generally the longest part of the sales process and requires the most effort by both the client and the salesperson. Anyone can do an effective greeting and warm-up. Within 30 minutes, an untrained person can be taught enough about timeshare to impart that knowledge to another person. And just about everyone can ask someone else to purchase his or her product. What distinguishes anyone from an effective salesperson is the discovery.

To begin with, if the salesperson has been sharing breakfast or lunch with the client, it is important to clear the area up before beginning. This, along with the salesperson changing their stance from relaxed and informal to more attentive and business-like, will give a clear signal that the business part of the presentation is about to begin.

A proper transition from the Warm-Up to the Discovery is 'Well, Mr and Mrs Client, as I told you earlier, I'd like to ask you some questions about your vacations. May we begin now?' and wait for a firm 'YES.' If for any reason, all the clients present do not respond with a clear 'YES,' the salesperson should not, under any circumstances, proceed. Rather, whatever issues that the client raises needs to be addressed at that time, before proceeding. Assuming the client has said a 'yes,' the salesperson, who by now should have a pen in hand and be sitting straight up, both feet on the ground, legs uncrossed, should begin by taking out whatever the resort has provided for this purpose.

Of course, there are times when clients will try to rush the salesperson through the steps, including the Discovery, by saying things such as, 'Oh, its OK, we know about timeshare, we don't want to waste any of your time, just show us the price' or 'Just so you know, we are only in here for the tickets, we're not going to buy anything, so just show us the model.' It is imperative for the salesperson to stay calm, cool and collected if this happens. Remember, the sales process is under the control of the salesperson, not the client.

There are as many variations on discovery forms as there are resorts. A thorough discovery consists of at least 20 questions and a thorough salesperson will ask at least two or three follow-up questions to at least 75% of those questions.

Discoveries are designed to get the salesperson asking and the client answering first-, second- and third-level questions. A first-level question is designed to get a straightforward, factual-based question answered.

First-level question – 'Mr and Mrs Client, where did you go on your last vacation?'

A second-level question is designed to get some more information about that fact and scratch the surface of the emotion behind the fact.

Second-level question – 'Ah, you went to the mountains of Tennessee. What made you choose that area?'

A third-level question is designed to discover the core feeling.

Third level question – 'So when you went mountain climbing and exploring there on your vacation, how did that make you feel?'

Finding out where the client went on vacation or would like to go on vacation does nothing to help the salesperson sell. Further, finding out what the client does on vacation does not give much more information either. Discovering what the client feels on vacation in this example may uncover a Dominant Buying Motive. The discovery of one Dominant Buying Motive, perhaps relaxing or exhilarating in this case, does not make for a sale. A wise salesperson will take notes on all the Dominant Buying Motives that are uncovered during this process and weave them together to put forth a convincing and emotional reason for the client to make a purchase at the end.

> **Key learning point 5.3**
> Third-level or feeling questions will likely lead to being able to uncover one or more Dominant Buying Motives.

As previously discussed, male salespersons should address each question first to the male client and then to the female client, vice versa for female salespersons. It is imperative to elicit answers from BOTH or in some cases ALL the clients at the sales presentation. It is also important to note that the salesperson should strive to get complete answers to questions and not to accept answers such as 'whatever he/she says' or 'I agree' as direct answers. More often than not, the quiet client, the one that the salesperson 'thinks' is buying into the timeshare all along will shoot down the decision to purchase at the end. Being quiet does not mean that the client is agreeing.

One must remember that every step of the sales process, and indeed, every question that is asked and answered serve the purpose of taking the salesperson one step closer to the sale; here is an example of a thorough 22-question discovery:

1. On a scale of 1–10, how important are vacations to you?

2. What do you like to do on vacation?

3. What is the number one reason you go on a vacation?

4. Do you feel that you deserve a vacation?

5. What are the three things that would make your vacation better?

6. How many nights on average do you stay in a hotel on vacation?

7. What are your standards or criteria for a hotel? What do you look for?

8. What do you expect to pay for one night in a hotel that meets your standards or criteria?

9. Do you generally drive or fly to your vacation? Have you ever cruised? Would you like to?

10. When you vacation, do you vacation by yourselves, with children, with other family members, with friends, etc.?

11. Who generally does the planning when it comes to vacation and when do you start making your vacation plans?

12. If you could go anywhere in the world on vacation, where would you go and what would you do there? (It is a good idea to ask each of the people at the presentation this question about another person. For instance, if there is a husband, wife and two children, it is interesting to go 'round robin' – ask one of the children 'If your Mom could go anywhere in the world on vacation, where would she go and what would she do when she got there?' and so on around the table.)

13. On a scale of 1–5, how feasible are those vacations for you in the next five years?

14. Is there anything at all that would prevent you from going on vacation next year? And the following year?

15. Where was the best place you've ever been on vacation? What did you do? Would you go back?

16. In the next 5–10 years, where else will you be going on vacation?

17. Did you go on vacation as a child with your parents? What did you get out of them (or what did you feel you missed)?

18. Have you ever been on a timeshare presentation before this one?

19. Did you choose to become an owner at that time?

20. What was the number one reason you chose to (or not to) get involved then? (Can also be phrased as 'What did you most like and most not like about the timeshare or the salesperson?')

21. What are the three most important things in your life?

22. Finally, what questions do you have or what would you like me to focus on so that you will be able to make an informed choice about purchasing with us here today?

Some hints and tips about a Discovery are as follows:

- Remember that the Discovery is the most important part of the sales process. The salesperson should ALWAYS do a thorough Discovery no matter what the client says or what the client's circumstances are.

- Slow down and be sure to let the client finish their answers and/or their trains of thought. All too often, salespersons are too eager to ask the next question so that they can begin to tell the client about the product.

- Never sell during the Discovery and never answer objections during the Discovery. The Discovery is NOT the time to sell anything; it is however the time to let the client talk and the salesperson take notes.

- Remember that the more the salesperson listens, the more the client will talk and the more useful will be the information gathered.

- A good salesperson will listen and agree with the client during the Discovery, even if it seems as if agreeing with the client will diminish the use of the product. People will always defend their stance more when they meet with resistance and will always find fault with their stance when they meet with agreement. If the salesperson tells the client that their way of going on vacation is 'wrong' in some way, the client will fight to death (figuratively of course) to defend their way of vacationing.

CASE STUDY

Mark is a new salesperson and has had no successful sales in his first 16 tours. He meets his clients and follows his manager's instruction; doing a great greeting, intent statement and warm-up.

He has 17 carefully worded Discovery questions and delves deeper into each one, asking great follow-up questions. When Mark asks questions about the clients' past vacations, Mark points out resorts in the directory and asks, 'Was your hotel as nice as this resort?' When he finds out that the clients like to cruise, he shows them that they can use the timeshare towards cruises.

Mark's manager notices that each time Mark talks about timeshare, his client's answers get shorter and their body language noticeably pulls back.

Reflective practice

1. Read the case study and comment on what Mark needs to work on.
2. If you were Mark's manager, what would be the #1 coaching tip you would offer to him?
3. Why are Mark's clients pulling away from him during the discovery?

Information confirmation

Immediately after the Discovery, the salesperson should sincerely thank each client for his or her time and input. The Information Confirmation step is a very simple and short step that is often overlooked, leading to a lack of trust and ultimately no sale.

The purpose of the Information Confirmation is simple – to let the client know that what they said was heard and understood. 'The client doesn't care how much you know, they know how much you care,' is a statement that sums up why an Information Confirmation is vital.

A good Information Confirmation sums up what the client has just told the salesperson WITHOUT having the salesperson sound like a recording. An effective salesperson will be able to sum up the 22 questions in a short narrative or concise story. It should be noted that emphasis is on the words 'short' and 'concise.' While the discovery may have taken 20 minutes, the Information Confirmation should not take more than 1.5–2 minutes and does not have to hit on every single question that has been asked.

Example

'Well Mr and Mrs Client, let me see if I have all of that…Mr Client feels that his vacations are about a 7 in importance and Mrs Client feels that they are about an 8 to her, and you both feel that you deserve a vacation. The number one reason you go on vacation is to get away from work and have some quality time with the family.

You both like to ski on vacation and Mrs Client likes to shop. You really enjoyed the trip you took last year to Cancun because it gave you a chance to get away from the cold back in Boston and you'd both like to go back again, although you'd like to try a cruise next time. Mr Client's dream vacation would be to sit on a beach and do nothing in Fiji and Mrs Client wants to go to Venice, Italy, because she's always heard how beautiful it was. You don't feel that either Fiji or Venice is something that you're going to be able to do within the next five years, because you feel that the children are too young right now, and you don't feel you have the money.

You typically vacation with the children and although it varies, your hotel accommodations are running you about $75 per night. Having more options, having less bad surprises and having vacations cost less would make your vacations better in the future. Mrs Client does most of the planning for the vacations and she was the one who booked this vacation on line. Other than a major emergency or health issues, nothing would prevent you from going on a vacation next year or the year after that.

You've been on two timeshare presentations before this one and although you both liked the resort and the fact that you could trade the timeshare for other places, you chose not to become an owner then because you felt that the cost was too high. And in order for you to make an informed choice about purchasing here with (name of resort) today, you want me to cover the cost, the 'hidden' fees, the difference between a fixed week and a point system and explain why so many people that you know haven't been able to get the exchange that they wanted.

How did I do? Did I get that all OK? Anything else I should know about?

Mr and Mrs Client now know that the salesperson has indeed heard and understood what they said and heard their words and thoughts played back. The salesperson has now given Mr and Mrs Client the opportunity to clarify anything as well as given them a break to get their thoughts on track; they now know what they need to focus on for the next steps.

As with other steps in the sales process, the salesperson should end the Information Confirmation with a question such as 'Is that right?' or 'Did I leave anything out?' or 'Is there anything else that I should know?' followed by another sincere 'Thank You' and perhaps a simple handshake to each of the clients.

SUMMARY

This chapter together with Chapter 6 explores a systematic approach to planning, organizing and processing sales of timeshare properties to potential owners. Current research suggests that 'try before you buy' involves quite a costly way of generating potential sales leads. The vast majority of people invited to spend time at a resort and attend a sales presentation are unlikely to make a purchase. Most countries and regions of the world require resort organizations to give a 'cooling-off' period between signing a contract and the contract becoming legal. This is recognition of the hard sales pressures that can be part of the sales trick. This generally allows people to rethink the contract they have signed during the sales presentation. It recognizes that some sales techniques can be **pressured and in a few cases dishonest**. Apart from the poor public relations impact this generates, it is wasteful in its use of selling time and resources. A systematic targeted approach is needed to produce a better conversion rate and more effective use of resources.

CHAPTER 6

The 12-Step Sales Process: Part 2

After working through this chapter, you should be able to understand the following:

- why it is essential to discover the vacation problem
- how to present the product features of the resort in a customized way
- the essential points of a proper closing
- the great consequences of a follow-up

INTRODUCTION

Chapter 5 pointed out the importance of a systematic approach to sales presentations. Even though most timeshare presentations are made to individuals who have no intention of making a purchase, some do have an intention to purchase if the package looks as though it meets their needs. This emphasizes the need for a professional, planned and empathetic approach to attract a better success rate. Certainly, research confirms that sales rates vary widely between those who are systematic and those who are not. The important point to keep in mind is that a successful sale results in the long-term settlement of the deal. It is in no one's interest for sales closures to result in rescissions later. Rescission is the term used to describe the process whereby customers who have agreed to a deal withdraw from it during the 'cooling-off' period. This chapter outlines the latter stages of the selling process.

PRESENTATION AND UNCOVERING OF PROBLEMS

People purchase timeshare because they want to gain something that is missing from their current vacation experience. It is the responsibility of the salesperson to uncover, and then, fix the client's vacation problem. What is a vacation problem and how to uncover it? Each person will have different answers and the easiest and quickest way to uncover the problem is for the salesperson to ask the simple question, 'What would make your past, present day and future vacations better?' and then remain quiet and wait for the answer.

A typical list may look like this:

- More space in the hotel room

- Cheaper vacations

- More vacations

- Longer vacations

- More things to do on vacation

Or clients may say that nothing would make their vacations better.

Obviously, the first scenario is the easy one to 'solve' with whatever timeshare you may be selling. The second one may indicate several things, the first being that the salesperson has not done an adequate job of warming up to the client and thereby 'earning' the right to ask questions that help sell the product.

The aim here is to get as much of the problem from the client, while at the same time, knowing that the timeshare product can solve the problem. For instance, if the client says that 'having more money would make my vacations better,' something of course that is not 'solvable' by owning a timeshare, the salesperson should probe more and ask, 'Well, let me understand…are you more interested in lower cost vacations or in higher value for the money you are already spending on vacation?' This will cause the consumer to think carefully while at the same time give salespersons enough information to tailor their presentation to the exact problem.

Getting the vacation problem out of the client however is not the end of this step. It is imperative for the salesperson to ask a question, very often in terms of a tie-down close.

> 'So Mr and Mrs Client, if I was able to show you something here today that would solve your vacation problems and let you continue to live your life the way you want to, is that something that you would be interested in getting involved with today?'

Or

> *'Thank you. So, let me ask you a question John and Mary…If, and I'm not saying that I have anything, but if we showed you something here today that solved all of your vacation problems that you've shared with me, and didn't take away from the rest of your life, is there any reason why you wouldn't become an owner with us here today?'*

Again, as with any other question that a salesperson asks during the course of the presentation, it is important to ask the question and then shut up and wait for the answer. Let the question sit, let the client think. Although it may seem like an eternity, don't jump in, don't rephrase the question, just sit and wait for the answer. Unless the salesperson receives a 'YES' for this question, there is no point moving ahead.

There are only two outcomes: The first is if the client answers 'YES.' In this case, the salesperson should thank the client, possibly shake their hand and move forward. The second and more likely scenario is if the client answers 'NO.' What is to be done then? Simply ask, 'No? Well, obviously you have a reason for saying that. Why do you feel that way?' At which point the client is likely to say something like, 'Well, we are buying a house and we don't have any money for a timeshare' or 'Well, we're saving for the kid's college education and every dollar we have goes into that fund' or 'No, we already have a timeshare and we are just here for the tickets.'

It is important for the salesperson to maintain composure, not get exasperated and not argue. A good salesperson will take a step back, assume there was some miscommunication on their part and simply rephrase the question, 'I'm so sorry John and Mary, I must not have been clear, what I was asking you is that if I was able to show you a way to solve all of your vacations and at the same time, allow you to buy that house (send the children to college, enhance the great timeshare you already have, etc.) is there any reason why you wouldn't want to take advantage of that today?' And again, shut up and wait for the answer.

Two things bear repeating here are as follows:

- There must be a vacation problem or several problems to solve or the client will not buy any timeshare.

- The salesperson must get a clear verbal confirmation from the client to the problem-solving question in order to continue

Key learning point 6.1

If the salesperson does not uncover a vacation problem that the client truly feels and takes possession of, no sale will be made.

Product features

Points or weeks, floating or fixed, right-to-use or deeded, the salesperson must show the client how the product solves or fixes the problem and give at least a general overview of the product. It is important to understand that although the salesperson may have accumulated 15 years of product knowledge, the client is not interested in a four-hour dissertation of time-share. Good salespeople will abide by this rule; 'Know everything you say, don't say everything you know.' Remember also that the message that you are trying to convey to the client is composed of only 7% verbal information, the remaining 93% coming from visual and vocal information.

During this stage of the sales process, the salesperson will introduce the timeshare product, show the features of the product that make sense for the individual consumer and demonstrate personal and company credibility. Regardless of whether the client has been through four timeshare presentations before this one, or whether this is the first, it is imperative that the salesperson gives and is able to back up his or her personal credibility and the credibility of the company. Basically, this sub-step is to answer the un-asked question from the client, 'Why should I buy this from you and from your company?'

Table 6.1 gives some examples of personal and company credibility topics. Credibility statements can, and oftentimes do, sound rehearsed which takes away their impact. A good salesperson will be able to do both a personal and a company credibility statement in no more than 60 seconds, while at the same time making it sound like a conversation, not like a rehearsed acceptance speech.

Major errors are made in this crucial Product Features step of the presentation. The most common errors come from the salesperson talking about features that are of no interest to the client, and raising objections that the client never had to begin with. Although it is true of course that there are

Table 6.1	Personal Credibility and Company Credibility

Personal

How long you have had your timeshare license
The fact that you own and use timeshare
How long you have been employed in the industry
The fact that you have won an ARDA award

Company

How long the resort has been in business
How many clients own at the resort
Any awards the resort may have won

numerous resorts in both Hawaii and Wisconsin available through both of the major exchange companies, showing your client one or both of these locations is not necessary and will be detrimental if the client has no interest in either of these places. An all too common error inexperienced salespeople make is telling the client about places that they, the salesperson, wants to vacation, or where they assume their client wants to vacation.

Another mistake salespeople make at this stage is giving the client the answer to every question before finding out why the client has asked this. 'Does every resort have a swimming pool?' is not a good time for the salesperson to answer 'yes' or 'no' as the case may be. Why is the client asking this question? Perhaps the client likes pools, perhaps they don't. Perhaps the client has an allergic reaction to chlorine; perhaps they are afraid that the resort will be noisy when children are allowed to dive into the pool.

'*Interesting question*. You obviously have a reason for asking that. May I ask why you asked?' is a great way of getting more information out of the client. This way, when the client answers, 'I don't like pools, they are noisy' the salesperson can answer with 'Well, one of the great features is that you are not assigned a specific villa, so when you make your reservations and you let the resort know, they will assign you a villa in a building away from the pools.'

Although the information that the salesperson presents during this phase of the presentation varies, there are a few basics that cannot be overlooked. These are as follows:

- the exchange company(ies) that the resort is affiliated with

- the fact that certain fees are applicable such as maintenance fees, exchange or usage fees, membership fees, etc. It is not necessary, nor recommended to get into specific numbers, but the client must know by the end of this step that there are fees associated with the purchase other than the purchase price

- how the client will use the product, both home use and exchanging

- a brief discussion of weeks or seasons as they pertain to owning and using the timeshare

- whether the timeshare is deeded, a right-to-use, fixed week based, floating week based, point based, etc. and what privileges that ownership gives the client (the ability to sell, will, etc.)

Note that the information should be presented in a conversational style and should always be tied back to the client's individual vacation wants and needs.

It is interesting to note that, only seven per cent of the message that the client receives is directly linked to verbal information. Part of the message that draws people in is sight. One resource that is oftentimes overlooked by salespeople, regardless of their level of experience, is the resort directory for the affiliated exchange company, for example RCI or II. It is full of lovely photos designed to give the clients a small glimpse into what sort of vacations they could be having.

The three sections of the book that should be used in every single presentation are as follows:

- several locations in the geographic area where clients went to on their last vacation – to compare where they stayed with, where they could have been staying

- the resort that the client is at now – as a prelude to the property that they are about to see for themselves in the following step

- several locations in the geographic area where the client wants to go to on their future vacations – to pre-emptively compare staying at one of those resorts to the 'average' hotel or motel that they might be staying in

Whatever feedback you get, carefully consider how you will answer and then lead them to the actual timeshare property.

CASE STUDY

Doug has read every book about sales techniques that he can and spends an hour a day reading up on the timeshare industry. He is always on time, dresses professionally and treats his clients with utmost respect.

Despite this, his closing percentage is only 4% and he is in danger of losing his job. He asks his manager to please help out and the manager decides to role-play with Doug.

He asks Doug the following questions while role-playing:

'Is there a lake on property?'

'Does the resort have any plans to expand?'

'Can I use this timeshare at other resorts?'

Doug answers all three questions correctly: yes, yes and yes.

Reflective practice

1. Read the case study and comment on Doug's answers.
2. What would be a better way of answering these same questions?
3. Discuss how giving answers too quickly may not be a good practice.
4. In what situations may the client NOT want to hear 'yes' to those questions?

PROPERTY VIEWING

Unless the resort is in the pre-construction stage, property viewing is one of the most important parts of the sales process and, ironically, the one step of the sales process that is either overlooked and/or misunderstood. Non-timeshare owning clients will most often be staying off-property, but in-house clients and in some cases non-timeshare owning clients will be staying on property, meaning that they have seen the physical resort, have seen the Jacuzzi in the room, have used the amenities already, etc. No matter what, the property should still be shown in the sales process.

What does a good property tour or viewing consist of? That of course depends on what the particular resort has to offer the clients combined with what the salesperson has discovered about the clients' need and wants. Some rules of thumb are as follows:

- The property tour should not be conducted like some 'Grey Line Bus Tour.' It is not just showing the pool area followed by saying, 'this is our Olympic-sized swimming pool' or showing the kitchen in the timeshare room, pointing out to the toaster and commenting, 'and you always get a toaster in your kitchen.'

- Don't point out details that you know your client is not interested in, and don't point out every single feature.

- Don't make the property viewing portion of the tour longer than necessary by showing or commenting on features that have no benefit, for example houses of famous (or infamous) people that are nearby, restaurants, golf courses or other amenities that aren't connected to the actual timeshare, etc.

- Remember that every feature you show your clients should have a corresponding benefit to them.

- Don't run through the property tour ... while it may be true that you, the salesperson have seen the property 1746 times, it is, in all likelihood, the client's first time.

- Let the clients put themselves in the picture. Showing the gym is not enough, using word pictures let the client see themselves using the equipment and elicit feedback on how that feels.

- Even if the client is staying on property, or if the client has stayed on property three times before, or if the client has friends who own there, the full property tour is still needed. The client's room is full of open suitcases and unmade beds. The client may be staying in a one-bedroom but has no idea what the three-bedroom looks like or conversely, may be staying in a three-bedroom but has no idea of what the one-bedroom looks like.

Here are two examples of what a portion of a property tour should consist of:

Walking into the kitchen

'Here at Brand X Resort, you'll notice that the kitchens come complete with plates, glasses and silver wear and if you look closely, you'll see that it's the same high quality that you have in your own home, isn't it? Mrs Client, you said earlier that you really don't like having to eat out three meals every single day on vacation because it gets to be a hassle and the kids never seem to be hungry when you are at the restaurant, but an hour later, they all get hungry. How would you make use of the kitchen…for full meals or for having snacks available?

Passing by the front desk

'One thing that I want to make sure you visit is our Front Desk. It looks like any other front desk of any other hotel. You see brochures of fun things to do in the area and there are professionals with name tags behind the counter. But, unlike the front desk of the hotel that you are staying at right now, when you check out, you don't have to pay anything. Your nominal exchange fee has already been taken care of before you arrived. Wouldn't that go a long way to eliminate some of the hassle of vacationing, Mr Client?'

At some point in the property tour, and before entering the sales environment again, the salesperson should ask at least one trial close question without putting any pressure on the client. Something as simple as, 'Can you see yourself vacationing like this here and in Las Vegas, (Branson, England, Hawaii, etc.)? Is there anything at all that would prevent you from becoming involved with us here today and taking advantage of this great system?'

Don't be afraid of asking the question. If the client is not given the opportunity to present objections or questions now, they will certainly bring them up after they have been shown a price. Good salespeople will welcome questions and objections throughout the presentation, including trial closes because it shows that the client is engaged.

The only thing that the client should bring up at this point is money, as in responding by saying 'Well, I'm sure it's too expensive.' or 'Like I told you before, we're buying a house right now and we can't afford anything.' Don't be tripped up by responses similar to this. The salesperson's job is to make the clients want the product, and see and feel themselves enjoying the product. If the only thing that the client brings up is the money, the salesperson has done their job up until now.

One final step before moving to the closing is to isolate the objection, that is make sure that the money (or whatever) is the **only** thing that stands in the way of the client owning the timeshare. 'Thank you for sharing Mr and Mrs Client. Let me understand, you would very much like to own this and the only thing that you are concerned about is the money, specifically being able to afford the house and the timeshare is that right?' Well, I can't promise anything, but if there was a way you could buy the house and enjoy vacations is there anything else that would prevent you from owning?'

Two things to notice in the above paragraph:

- 'and' instead of 'but' as in '...much like to own this **and** the only thing...' The word 'and' means a continuation of the preceding statement. The word 'but' means an interruption or in more direct terms, negates what has come before.

- 'own', 'enjoy vacations' and 'own' instead of 'buy' or 'purchasing'. The word 'buy' can be a negative trigger for many clients. It can bring to mind outlaying of money, paperwork, etc. All of which will arise, but should be put off until the client has made the choice to own.

> **Key learning point 6.2**
> Although using certain key words and/or phrases is not sufficient to cause a sale, it is sufficient to cause the loss of a possible sale.

Solution of the problem

At this point, the client should be in a receptive mood. They've just seen the timeshare, spent at least 90 minutes getting to know the salesperson and the product and had their questions answered. Many salespeople make the deadly mistake of taking the client back and immediately try to sell or close the client. Instead, it is important for the client to understand and confirm that what they have just seen, will in fact, solve their vacation problems. The salesperson should take out the piece of paper where they (or the client) had listed all of the vacation problems and go over each and every one of them to insure that the timeshare will indeed solve all of the problems that the client indicated they had.

It may go something like this ... 'Well, I'm glad you enjoyed seeing the property. Before I give you the opportunity to become involved with us, let's first make sure that this does solve your earlier vacation problems. Mary, you said that having bigger hotel rooms was a problem for you. How would owning here solve that problem for you?' Again, ask the question and let Mary speak and finish completely. The salesperson is many times in a rush to get to the money, but many times the client simply needs time to process the information and tie the new information (the timeshare) to the old information (the problem.) 'John, you indicated earlier that lower cost vacations would make things better. Which part of the lower cost vacations do you like better, the savings in having a kitchen wherever you go on vacation, or the fact that you can stay in condos anywhere in the world for a fraction of what you would pay as a renter?' 'And John and Mary, you both said that you would like to go on more vacations, but sometimes find it difficult to get a good hotel room nearby...how would owning this solve that for you?' And so on down the entire list of vacation problems.

Closing

There are two ways that resorts and salespeople handle closing. One is where the salesperson does the entire procedure; start to finish, often referred to as 'front to back.' The other way is for the salesperson to stop here and let the sales manager handle the pricing and asking for the money. New salespeople often do not like the closing, or asking for the money, preferring to handle everything up until the pricing. Many resorts do not give the salesperson access to inventory, pricing, etc., mandating that a manager or a TO (short for Take Over) handle the pricing and the closing. We will discuss managers and TOs in a later section.

A majority of resorts insist that the salesperson and/or the sales manager show the client a fake price. In the car business, this is referred to as the 'sticker price.' Although it is true that some clients like to negotiate or haggle over the price, with clients having more and more access to information, including average pricing of timeshares and most clients at this point having gone through two or more timeshare sales presentations at some point in the past, most clients prefer the salesperson to be straightforward with the pricing.

Front to back

Once the salesperson and client have gone over everything including the solution of the vacation problem, including the various trial closes and/or tie-down closes, the only thing left to do is present the price and close the deal. It is important for the 'front to back' salesperson to remember all that they have uncovered from the presentation and 'marry' it together with the products that the timeshare resort has to offer, that is the different sizes, seasons, weeks, point values, etc.

The easiest way to begin to discuss the price of the timeshare is for the salesperson to do another tie-down close followed by the hotel rental dollar figure that was discussed early on. 'Well, Mr and Mrs Client, I'm sure that by now you see why so many people own timeshare, and how it can solve all of the vacation problems you told me about earlier, don't you? Now, earlier, you told me that you typically spend $15,000 per year on your vacation accommodations and that since you wanted to continue to vacation at least this much every year for the next X years, you were going to spend $15,000 anyway, isn't that right? So, let me show you how you can own this type of quality vacation accommodation every year for only $15,000.'

Table 6.2 shows a typical price sheet. Several things may happen at this point, and the client may have an objection about the following:

(a) the total price

(b) the annual fees

(c) the financing terms

(d) the down payment

(e) the monthly payment

(f) the issue of purchasing today

(g) the entire purchase

There are significant differences between an objection, an excuse and a condition. For now, let us continue and focus on the presumption that the only true objection the client has to do with is money. If the client were to say, 'Well, $15 000 is a lot of money' there is no need for the salesperson to say anything. Saying that $15 000 is a lot of money is NOT an objection, it is a statement. The client has not said that they don't have the money, or that $15 000 is more than they make in a year, or that $15 000 is more than what they would spend in 15 lifetimes of vacations. It is merely a comment. The astute salesperson will sit back quietly and observe. As in other parts of the presentation, the first person to say anything after this is at a disadvantage. Someone will eventually speak up; let the client say something, anything first before responding.

The client may follow up with 'And we don't have $15,000 as a down payment today.' NOW, the salesperson may enter and say something such as,

Table 6.2   Price Sheet

ACME Resort Purchase Proposal

Date_____   Tour Number_____   Market Source_____

Purchaser Name_____   SSN_____

Purchaser Name_____   SSN_____

Address_____

City/State/Zip Code_____

Country_____   E-Mail Address_____

Home Phone_____   Work Phone_____

Occupancy Year_____   O/E_____   Points_____   Season_____   Unit_____

Price_____ $_____

Less First Visit Incentive_____ $_____

Total Price_____ $_____

Closing Cost_____ $_____

Membership Fee_____ $_____

Down Payment_____ $_____

Form of Payment_____

Amount Financed_____ $_____

Interest Rate_____   # of Months Financed_____   Annual Fees $_____

Monthly Payment_____   Beginning_____   Ending_____

Auto Debit Checking_____   Auto Debit Credit Card_____   Payment Book_____

Notes:_____

_____

_____

Purchaser   Purchaser

Salesperson   Sales Manager   Verification Officer

'So, the down payment of $x is the only thing that would stop you from
owning this today?' At this point, the client may agree that yes, the only thing
that would stop them is the down payment or add something else to the
objection such as the monthly payment. Let's assume that the down
payment of $x is in fact the only objection that the client brings up. The front
to back salesperson must now draw on their knowledge of the resort's policies, that is they must know how much of the down payment must be paid
today and how long the client has to pay the remainder of the down payment.

'Well, Mr and Mrs Client, how much of the down payment would you be
willing to put down today? Would half of $x work for you if we gave you until
the end of the month to send in the remainder?' Notice the use of the phrase
'would you be willing to put down today' as opposed to 'how much can you
afford' or 'how much would be comfortable for you.' The answer to either of

those phrases is 'nothing' because 'nothing' is a quick and easy answer to the question of affordability or comfort.

It is important at this point to discuss the advantages of showing the client two distinct different price sheets, known as an alternate close. The benefit of an alternate close is that the client has a choice of saying 'yes' to one of two timeshare products at different prices, or the choice of saying 'no' to the only timeshare product being shown. Look at it as a 'YES' 'YES' or a 'YES' 'NO.' In the first case, the client has to say, 'YES' to something that the salesperson has shown. In the latter case, the client can say, 'YES' to the product or 'NO' to the product.

If the salesperson has done their job correctly and the client is in fact capable of purchasing (mainly a marketing issue) the only objection that should occur at this point will relate to the affordability of the product in terms of either the down payment or the monthly payment. Even if the salesperson is capable of going 'front to back' it sometimes is a good idea to bring in a sales manager or a TO (Take Over) as a second face to back up what the salesperson has said, to answer a question that the client has (even if the salesperson is more than capable of correctly answering the question), or to handle distinct money questions.

Using a sales manager

If the resort mandates using a sales manager, a/k/a as a 'TO' for 'Take Over,' the salesperson should do everything as discussed before, including the tie-down close and then bring a manager to the client to handle the closing. As just mentioned, sometimes it behooves the salesperson to bring in a manager to handle specific money issues such as down payment or monthly payment. Either way, the manner in which the sales manager or TO is introduced to the client is extremely important and an ineffective, weak or messy TO transfer can sometimes lose a deal for the salesperson. A manager is brought over to help both the client and the salesperson, both literally and psychologically.

The salesperson has a very short time to give the manager the pertinent information about the clients; their vacation likes and dislikes, where the client is from, where and how the clients would use the product and what if any, are the client's objections. A proper TO transfer should go something like this (With the salesperson standing): 'Mr and Mrs Client, this is Ms Lake, my manager.' The salesperson should now sit down on their chair, which they have moved to the client's side – the male salesperson sitting next to the male client and vice versa for female salespersons. 'Ms Lake, Mr and Mrs Client are visiting us from Illinois. They have seen timeshare before, and really like our product because of the flexibility and because they often come here on vacation. Mr Client wants to vacation in South Carolina so that he can play golf and Mrs Client really wants to go to Hawaii to see the volcanoes. They would love to own here, and the only issue they have is the down payment. $x is a bit too much for them right now – $500 works for them. How can you help us?'

Notice a few things in that transfer:

(a) The use of the word 'and' instead of the word 'but' as in 'and the only issue they have.' The reason is simple but important…the word 'but' literally means 'discard everything I have said before this, what I'm about to say now is really the truth,' which is not what the salesperson wants to put forth.

(b) The fact that 'affordable' and/or 'comfortable' was not used.

(c) The use of the word 'how' in 'How can you help us?' assumes that the manager will help; it doesn't ask whether the manager can help.

(d) The use of the word 'us.' The salesperson has aligned themselves with the client by the subtle move of the chair closer to the client when the manager was introduced, and now verbally by the word 'us' meaning the clients AND the salesperson.

Follow-up

As you can see, selling timeshare is not the easiest process. It takes careful preparation, knowledge, understanding of psychology and a bit of luck. A good salesperson will receive a 'yes' at the end of the presentation approximately 15% of the time…a stellar salesperson approximately 25% of the time. This final step, follow-up, is key to keeping those sales and ultimately

CASE STUDY

Mr and Mrs Brehmer bought their first timeshare while on vacation in the Wisconsin Dells. When they returned home to Chicago two days later, they looked through all the paperwork and started asking themselves whether they had made the right choice.

After seven days of questioning themselves and not hearing anything from the timeshare resort and/or Judy, their salesperson, whose card they had lost, they decided to exercise their right of recession and cancelled the timeshare purchase.

One month later, Judy noticed that she did not get paid on the deal and questioned the payroll department about it. She was informed that the Brehmers had cancelled their purchase.

'I'm so surprised to find this out,' Judy said, 'we had such good rapport and I was so sure that they really wanted it.'

Reflective practice

1. What could Judy have done to prevent the Brehmers from cancelling their contract?
2. What could other resort personnel do to prevent the Brehmers from cancelling their contract?
3. How likely are the Brehmers to refer the timeshare resort to friends and co-workers?
4. What types of follow-up would consumers appreciate?

getting paid on them. As we've discussed earlier, the timeshare industry has not made a move to insure that timeshare is a sought after product. Therefore, most, if not all, of the purchasers will suffer from some sort of buyer's remorse after purchasing. A good salesperson will know this, empathize with their clients and understand what is needed to keep the sale, insure the client is happy with the purchase and that the client refers others.

SUMMARY

Although the timeshare product has changed and improved over the years, its ultimate success or failure is in the hands of a salesperson. Through understanding the consumer's mindset and clearly demonstrating excellent social, questioning and listening skills, a salesperson will be able to demonstrate the features of the timeshare product which will solve one or more of the client's vacation problems.

CHAPTER 7

Points Versus Weeks

After working through this chapter, you should be able to

- understand the difference between fixed versus float timeshare weeks.

- understand the difference between a deeded and a right-to-use timeshare.

- understand the evolution of the timeshare industry and how it has changed how the timeshare product is used.

- recognize the difference between the timeshare week system and the timeshare point system.

INTRODUCTION

As the timeshare industry has evolved so has the timeshare product. It has grown to offer many different features and manifests in many different ways. This chapter will cover the different types of timeshare products offered by both independent and brand companies. The complexity of the timeshare product is a result of the many different types of experiences that is now being offered. The 'cookie cutter' is a product of the past, and this chapter will help the reader understand all of the different types of timeshares and the terminology related to the product.

CONTENTS

FIXED TIMESHARE WEEKS

When the first timeshare was developed in Europe in the 1960s, the idea was simple. Each condominium unit was divided into 52 weeks and sold. The person that bought a week in a particular unit would own that week and be able to return to the condominium and stay in that unit during that same week year after year. By definition, a Fixed week timeshare is a timeshare plan under which the purchaser receives a specific use period (usually a unit week) in a specific unit that the purchaser is entitled to use each calendar year without making a prior reservation. The cost of the week would be based on the size of the unit (studio, one, two, or three bedrooms) and the time of year the week was purchased (a week purchased at a beach timeshare during the summer would cost more than one purchased during the winter at the same resort). This concept is still in place at some timeshare resorts and is commonly referred to as a Fixed Week.

Type of ownership: deeded versus right-to-use

The type of timeshare ownership that has remained continuous throughout the years is how they are owned. The first type is fee simple or deeded where the owner actually owns a fraction of the unit and the common property of the resort. Once the cost of the timeshare is fully paid, the owner gets title to a fraction of the unit and can will it to their family or friends upon their death. For a one-time purchase price and payment of a yearly maintenance fees and taxes, the owner possesses their vacation either in perpetuity or for a predetermined number of years.

The other type of ownership is the right-to-use where the owner is entitled to use a unit at a resort for a specified period of time (it could be once a year for 20 years). The owner buys the property with a right to use but does not have an ownership interest. With a right-to-use type of timeshare resort, the ownership of the resort remains with the developer. The purchaser reserves the right to use one or more resort weeks for a specified number of years. The length of right-to-use timeshare plans generally ranges from 10 to 50 years. After the agreement is completed, the rights to the property return to the developer. The right-to-use membership does have different forms, but the most common one is the destination club membership which will be discussed in Chapter 13.

The concept of right to use is like joining a country club. To be a member, a person has to pay a membership fee and then pay dues to continue their membership, and for this, they have the right to use the facilities (Vacation Ownership, 2008). However, they own nothing if the country club goes bankrupt; they have no legal rights. The same is true with a right-to-use ownership of a timeshare. If the timeshare goes bankrupt, the timeshare has no value. The right-to-use concept is commonly in practice in countries where it is illegal or difficult for foreign citizens to own land. The result of both types of ownership is that ownership entitles the owner to a certain amount of time in the purchased property per year. Owners of the timeshare share both the use and the costs of upkeep of the timeshare and the common grounds of the resort property (Vacation Ownership, 2008).

The owner of a deeded timeshare resort can either use their week themselves, give it to friends or family to use, rent the week, or leave it vacant as long as they are up to date on their payments (if they are still making them on the cost of the timeshare) and their maintenance fees. The right to-use may have restricted access to the owner renting or giving away the owner's week depending on the terms of the right-to-use membership.

FLOAT TIMESHARE WEEKS

During the 1970s and 1980s, the timeshare industry grew, and with this growth came the desire for more than owning one week at one resort and returning every year. The timeshare resort developers found that a way to solve this problem was to offer float memberships. The owner would not be buying just one week that they would return to every year. They would be buying a week in a season or a week during a year. For instance, in the timeshare industry, the weeks are numbered 1–52. A person that buys a fixed week would buy a certain week say week 1 and they would own week 1 for as long as they owned the timeshare, and if it was a deeded timeshare, they would pass on their timeshare and week 1 to whomever they willed the timeshare to.

Float timeshares are bought with the understanding that the person must make a reservation ever year to stay in their timeshare week. This is done by choosing the season (Spring, Summer, Fall, Winter), by week number (e.g. weeks 1–16, 17–32, 33–52) or by year (choice of any week during the calendar year). With the floating timeshare concept, there is an increase in flexibility coupled with the increase that owners may not receive the week they desire. By definition, a Floating week timeshare is a timeshare plan under which the purchaser receives a timeshare interest in the plan subject to the requirement that the purchaser contacts the association or management company to reserve a specific use period in a specific unit each calendar year. At this time, approximately 70 per cent of timeshare resorts in the United States are sold as float week timeshares (Vacation Ownership, 2008).

It is essential that the distribution of weeks be done fairly. Some time-share resorts charge more for the season or weeks that are more desirable to make certain that demand is managed properly. Some timeshare resorts incorporate what is called breakage. Breakage is a use period which has not been reserved by any timeshare owner before the commencement of the use period or a specifically defined breakage period. Breakage is the term often used by the management company for maintenance or by the management company or the developer for use in a rental program. Having a breakage week or weeks is necessary for maintaining units and can also be used for special events that are very popular (e.g. Mardi Gras in New Orleans). If the owner knows in advance that certain weeks cannot be used by a time-share owner, it is legal to withhold those weeks for rentals. This takes away the headache of frustrated owners not getting to use popular weeks; however, the timeshare will not be worth as much to some, so the development company will have to charge less for the timeshare.

FIXED VERSUS FLOAT

There is no 'better' timeshare to buy when it comes to the fixed versus float timeshare plan. If a person intends to use the resort where they buy at the same time every year and if it is important to get back to the resort the same time every year (e.g. first week of the year for skiing at New Year's at a skiing resort) then a Fixed week would be a better option. If you do not want to be tied down to one week at the same time every year, then the Float week would be a better option. One is not necessarily more or less expensive than the other. For example, if someone bought a holiday week at a resort that had a Fixed timeshare plan, it would cost more than if a person was going to the same area and purchased at another resort that had a Float plan. However, if the person owned a Fixed week during the off season, they would be paying less than a person staying at another resort that had a Float plan.

Biennials

Biennial ownership is also called alternate year ownership. If a person does not have the time or the money to purchase one week of timeshare, they are given the option to purchase a biennial ownership. The timeshare owner will be able to use the resort every other year at a more affordable price.

Split weeks

Split weeks offered by timeshare resorts face the issue of the preference of shorter vacations by American tourists. A report by the Travel Industry of

America indicated that 80 per cent of trips taken in the United States are for two nights or less in duration (Travel Industry of America, 2008). This is based on the busy lifestyle of dual-income households that have a hard time taking a full week of vacation at one time. The split week gives the owner the ability to split use of the timeshare week into two separate visits to the resort, usually a one three-night and one four-night stay at two different times of the year. The reservations for split weeks are usually based on availability and not normally allowed during holidays or special events.

Lock-off units

Timeshare owners like the idea of spacious accommodations which is why the most popular size of accommodation is the two-bedroom timeshare unit (ARDA, 2008). The timeshare owner who may hesitate about purchasing a two-bedroom timeshare unit was given a solution, the lock-off unit. The lock-off timeshare was created when it was purpose built (built for the purpose of being a timeshare) with two entrances. A two-bedroom timeshare unit could become a studio and a one-bedroom condominium with the right design (or some other configuration based on the offer of the resort). The idea is that an owner could buy a two-bedroom timeshare unit and stay in the unit one year and if they decided the next year they could go on two different vacations at the timeshare resort. The owner would be staying one week in the studio of the lock-off unit and one week in the one-bedroom condominium portion of the unit. In essence, the owner would be getting two vacations for the purchase of one two-bedroom timeshare while only paying the maintenance fees for one timeshare unit.

Key learning point 7.1

Timeshare resorts have grown past their roots in Europe. What was once an inflexible product has become a product that allows a timeshare owner to pick the time of the year in which to vacation as well as the type of accommodations they desire.

CASE STUDY

Jeff and Pam Malloy have decided that they are interested in purchasing a timeshare. They are from Ohio and enjoy escaping the harsh winters in Florida once a year. They also enjoy playing golf and want to make certain that their timeshare resort has a quality golf course. They have school-aged children, so they need to work their vacations around their schedules. They really do not have a preference about when to vacation at their timeshare resort except that they want to vacation in the winter.

Reflective practice

1. What type of timeshare would you suggest they buy?
2. What would be the benefits and drawbacks between choosing a Floating timeshare week and a Fixed timeshare week?

HOME RESORTS

As timeshare resorts grew, developers built multiple timeshare resorts in different locations. To make timeshares more flexible, owners in timeshare resorts that had both fixed and floating week plans created the opportunity to exchange their week with another week at another property owned by the timeshare company. The exchange is on a first-come, first-serve basis during a certain time period. If the owner did not get the week they desired, they would get a week at the resort where they owned, their Home Resort.

In a multisite timeshare plan or exchange program context, the Home Resort is defined as a timeshare resort in which a purchaser owns a timeshare interest. The owners' home resort is used in determining maintenance fee obligations and priority use rights in reservation systems. For instance, if one owned a timeshare in Florida, it would be less expensive than if they owned a timeshare in Hawaii, because of the higher cost of maintaining a timeshare resort in Hawaii. If a person exchanges their timeshare at their home resort to go to a different resort in a particular year, they still would pay the maintenance fees at their home resort regardless of where they spent their time.

An owner's home resort is important in a situation where there is a Float week plan. An owner is given reservation priority at their home resort, meaning that they will be able to make reservations before anyone who does not own at the resort. The length of time can vary generally; it is either one or two months. Owners of a Float week resort who choose to stay at their home resort during their use year should make their reservations during this priority period to help ensure that they get the desired week.

Banking versus borrowing

Another option that came over time was to be able to use one's week in a different year. If for some reason you could not go on vacation in a particular year, you could bank your week and take a two-week vacation the following year. Banking is defined as the act of a timeshare owner in deferring the use of a timeshare interest from a given year into the next succeeding year. Also, if you want to go on a two-week vacation this year, you could borrow your week from the next year. Borrowing is defined as the act of a timeshare owner in using a timeshare interest from the next succeeding year in the current year.

Exchange programs

Exchange programs came about as the increase in the number of timeshares gave companies more options to deliver to their owners. If a timeshare developer built more than one property and created an exchange agreement between the properties, the owners would be able to have more flexibility in their timeshare ownership. The developer would create exchange programs for the purpose of these exchanges. An exchange program is defined as the contractual arrangement between a developer, an association, or a timeshare owner and an exchange company which enables the timeshare owners at that affiliated resort to exchange the use of their timeshare interests with that of other affiliated resorts.

The owner could deposit their week into the exchange program, and if another week was available at an affiliated resort, they could stay there instead of where they owned their timeshare. Deposit is defined as the transfer of use rights in a use period for a given use year into an exchange program. The success of these exchange programs led to the creation of Exchange companies which will be discussed in further detail in Chapter 8.

Timeshare resort companies have also realized that the more choices the timeshare owner has, the more appealing the product is. Some timeshare resort companies form affiliations with other properties so that the owners can exchange without going through the exchange company programs.

> **Key learning point 7.2**
>
> The use of other resorts as an owner benefit is a very popular option. However, as timeshare ownership has grown more complex, so has the planning to ensure that the timeshare owner is happy with what they have purchased. Delivering on the expectations that are created during the sale is essential for a satisfied timeshare owner.

> **Reflective practice**
>
> 1. How important do you think where a person purchases their timeshare is in terms of being happy with their purchase?
> 2. In what ways does the lack of knowledge or comprehension of the different types of programs mars the interaction between the owner and the resort?
> 3. What can be done to better educate the timeshare owner to make them feel that they are getting the most out of their timeshare purchase?

Timeshare usage options

Before the timeshare point system was created by the industry, the following usage options had been created by the timeshare industry.

1. Use the timeshare by staying at the owner's home resort.

2. Exchange it for another villa someplace else.

3. Loan it to family or friends.

4. Space bank it for future use if the owner cannot use it.

5. Borrow a week if the owner wants to go on a longer vacation.

6. Rent it out when the owner is not using it (Vacation Ownership, 2008).

The product had become more flexible, but some companies looked at ways to further expand the options provided for potential owners.

Timeshare versus points: overview

A problem that some timeshare owners have faced in the past is they found that they thought the timeshare they purchased was too complex. They did not understand how to best use their timeshare week so they could get their ideal vacation. The owners were looking for a simple way to use and exchange their week. From floating timeshare plans, lock-offs, and split weeks, the point system was born. The idea behind the point system was to give the timeshare owner the ability to increase the way they can make use of their timeshare week with ease. In a timeshare resort where you purchase a timeshare week, the timeshare owner would use the week to bank it, rent it, use it, or exchange it. The point system extends what owners can do with their week.

If a timeshare resort decides that they will operate as a point-based resort, they will figure out the value of each week in dollars and convert the week into points. Each resort has a different value for their point system. (There is only one point system that is recognized by a large group of resorts and that is the RCI point system; this will be discussed later in the chapter). The average price of a timeshare is currently $18 502 (ARDA, 2008). So it is possible that a resort sells a week of timeshare at a resort in North Carolina for $18 502. If it is a deeded resort, the owners would get a deed at the resort for a certain unit and a certain week that would be valued at that price. They may never stay in the unit during that week ever, but the resort has to sell points that are tied to an actual value or the points would be worth nothing.

When a person purchases points at a deeded timeshare resort, they get a deed and points to use every year. So the person buys the timeshare at a point-based resort in North Carolina and they spend $18 502, which gives them 300 points to use every year. With these 300 points, they will be able to stay in a two-bedroom condominium during their high season. A point system is a form of vacation ownership in which a person owns a certain number of points each year that represents the size of the unit and the season which you may use the timeshare unit. However, one can use the points in many different ways. A person that owns 300 points in a two-bedroom in North Carolina during high season may only need to use 100 points to stay at the same resort in a studio during low season or at a different resort in a one-bedroom during high season. Also, many resorts give the owners the opportunity to stay at a resort for as short as one night, so the owner could use their points to stay at their resort in North Carolina during high season in a three-bedroom timeshare unit for 100 points a night. Banking and borrowing programs are also offered in the point system, so the same person who wanted a three-week vacation at their North Carolina timeshare could bank 300 points one year and borrow 300 points another year and stay three weeks in a two-bedroom timeshare during high season during the year in between. The banking system also gives the owner the ability to 'roll over' points to the next year.

Benefits of point-based clubs

Point-based clubs or programs give the owner the opportunity to use accommodations in multiple resort locations and different sizes units at these locations. The point system benefits both owner and developer by letting the owner start small with a lower number of points and add on points as the need arises. An owner may begin owning enough points to book a one-bedroom during low season at the beginning of their membership and work their way up to owning enough points to book a four-bedroom presidential suite during high season. Points allow an increase in flexibility, letting the owner choose the length of stay (some programs allow the owner to stay at the resort for one night), size of unit, season of visit (high or low demand), and of course the destination. With these products, club members purchase points, which represent either a travel and use membership (right to use) or a deeded real-estate product.

There are many different point-based timeshare resorts and timeshare exchange programs available in the market today. The points are not inter-changeable among companies. If you own Hilton Grand Vacation points, you cannot use them at the Disney Vacation Club. The number of points that the owner purchases will determine the amount of vacation 'currency' that is deposited into their account each year. At the beginning of each year, the owner will receive a brand new set of points to use for their vacations. Similar to week-based programs, an owner can bank or borrow points from year to year.

Point-based resorts also help developers encourage owners to 'trade up.' In a country with limited vacation time after an owner buys one or two weeks of timeshare, they see no need to buy more. However, if they are part of a point-based program where they can buy more points to book a presidential suite, the attraction to purchase more is inherit.

Examples of point-based products

Disney Vacation Club

The Disney Vacation Club (DVC) was created in 1991 by Disney Vacation Development, Inc., a subsidiary of the Walt Disney Company. The Disney Vacation Club is a point-based membership product. The Disney Vacation Club is unique in that its membership, for most properties, will end on January 31, 2042. Membership at Saratoga Springs Resort and Spa will end on January 31, 2054 and that at the Animal Kingdom Villas will end on January 31, 2057. Although the owner is buying a 'real-estate interest' and the purchase is actually deeded, the ownership ceases to exist after these dates.

The Disney Vacation Club has a minimum number of points for an initial purchase of 160 points. The owner only buys the points once and they are renewed every year until the end of the contract.

The Disney Vacation Club point system is like any other point system in that it is demand based; a two-bedroom will cost more points than a one-bedroom. 'Weekday stays use less points than weekend stays. Booking a week in a studio at the Old Key West Resort in July will use more points (109) than booking that same size unit during January (80). Owners are supplied with easy to understand point charts and, with a little planning, points can be stretched a long way' (AllEars.net, 2008).

The Disney Vacation Club is operated based on use years. The use year begins as soon as points are purchased. So if an owner purchases in August, their use year begins in August, and this is when they will have access to a new set of points each year.

Disney Vacation Club owners can use their points in different ways. First by staying at Disney Vacation Club properties located in Florida, South Carolina, and properties that are under construction in Hawaii and

California. Second, points may be used to stay at all of the Disney lodging properties around the world located at Disney theme parks. Third, points may be used to book Disney cruises. Fourth, points may be used to book adventures (e.g. safaris or cruises to Alaska). Fifth, points may be used to stay at hotels in their concierge collection (e.g. Loews Regency Hotel, New York). Sixth, points may be used to stay at timeshare resorts around the world using their World Passport collection.

The home resort is the Disney Vacation Club resort where the owner first bought their points. The home resort advantage is that an owner can book their stays on their home property up to 11 months in advance, as opposed to seven months ahead for other Disney Vacation Club resorts. The four month window ensures that the home resort owners will get to book at their home resort.

Disney Vacation Club will let their owners bank and borrow points. Their policy is as follows: 'any unused vacation points into the upcoming use year can be banked or from the next use year can be borrowed. No more than three years of points can be combined at any one time. There are time limits on when banking is allowed, and once banked or borrowed, points cannot be returned to their original use year' (AllEars.net, 2008).

There has been an increase in the services offered to members of vacation clubs in order to help the membership become the 'one stop shopping' for travel plans and a members club offering special services. Disney Vacation Club Members have access to toll-free vacation planning through member services. 'Member Services can help with flights, car rentals, room requests and Priority Seating for meals. They are also available to assist in booking Member Getaway vacations, to arrange for groceries to be delivered to a members 'room' (AllEars.net, 2008).

Disney Vacation Club members have pool-hopping privileges at selected pools at the Disney resort when they are not at capacity. Members also receive discounts on the following: golf, shopping, spa treatments (at Saratoga Springs) and annual passes. Dining discounts at select restaurants are occasionally offered (usually 10–20%), room discounts at Disney resorts, and discounted tickets are available for Disney Quest, Pleasure Island and the water parks.

Hilton Grand Vacation Club

The Hilton Grand Vacation Club was created in 1992 with a point-based program. It is similar to the Disney Vacation Club in that the points are demand based, and the number of points that are owned determine the type of vacations that an owner can choose to go on. It is different from the Disney Vacation Club because Hilton Grand Vacation Owners own their points without an end date after which they will no longer own them. When an owner buys points, the number they own is based on their home resort, season when they purchased, and size of the villa they purchased.

As a Hilton Grand Vacation Club owner, they can use their points in the following ways: at their home resort or at any of Hilton Grand Vacation Club resorts or affiliated resorts, depositing points with Resort Condominiums International (RCI) and stay at an RCI affiliated resort worldwide, make last minute reservations with open season reservations with the Hilton Grand Vacation Club or RCI (stays are offered at a discount), an owner can bank or borrow points for additional vacation opportunities, convert points to Hilton Honors points (use for hotel stays, car rentals, airline tickets, etc.), reserve stays at Hilton properties worldwide and use the points for the club perks program that includes opportunities such as cruises, houseboats, RVs, and motorcycle travel. There are adventure travel opportunities such as hiking, biking and rafting as well (Hilton Grand Vacation Clubs, 2008).

RCI points

RCI points is a tool used by the RCI exchange company. Members are part of either RCI weeks or RCI points. If they are members of RCI weeks, they can deposit their week and exchange it for another week somewhere else in the world. RCI points was created to meet the demand of consumers seeking flexibility.

'As with all external timeshare exchange programs, the exchange company does not actually sell ownership at their affiliated resorts or memberships to their exchange company to those who do not own timeshare. To become a member of a timeshare exchange company, must first purchase timeshare ownership at an affiliated resort'" (Resort Condominiums International, 2008).

After an owner purchases with an RCI affiliated resort and the owner decides to be a part of the RCI point system, their week is assigned a point value to use in the RCI point system. The value is based on the following: resort location, resort ranking (in the RCI system), unit size, and season.

The owner that uses the RCI point system receives the following benefits (Resort Condominiums International, 2008):

- Dual RCI membership – points members can stay at ANY RCI Affiliated Resort – Points or Weeks.

- Choose the time of year they travel.

- Choose the size of the unit for each vacation.

- Stay for as short as one night.

- Save and borrow points to create dream vacations.

- Use points for more than just your vacation accommodations with RCI Point Partners: Cruises, Hotels, and Car rentals.

- Can avail of unlimited extra vacations at exclusive rates for RCI Members who don't use any points at all.

Key learning point 7.3

The timeshare point system has opened up many opportunities for the timeshare owner. However, with these opportunities has come the need to provide a greater education for the timeshare owner so they can get the most out of their timeshare ownership.

CASE STUDY

Sarah and Jeff Carter have two little girls that are 6 and 2 years old. They are very active travellers and they are looking to purchase a timeshare. They like going to the beach and to the mountains and cannot determine where the best place would be to buy their timeshare. They work their schedules around their oldest girls' schedule so they do not want to get locked into one week.

Charles and Jenny Howard are looking to purchase a timeshare as well. They love going to the beach and make plans to go for the 4th of July celebration at their favourite beach in Florida every year. They want to make certain that they can lock in a week over the 4th of July weekend so they can return to their timeshare every year at the same time.

Reflective practice

1. What type of timeshare would you suggest that Sarah and Jeff purchase?

2. What type of timeshare would you suggest that Charles and Jenny Howard purchase?

3. Would both couples be happy with the same kind of timeshare product? Yes or No and Why?

SUMMARY

The evolution of the timeshare industry has opened up different possibilities for the timeshare owner. The original product has grown into a diverse travel planning programme. The diversity of the product has made it more appealing to a larger market. As the product continues to evolve and meet the needs of a more receptive market, it is imperative that potential owners are educated about what timeshare would be best to fit their needs. The education process should continue throughout their ownership to ensure that the owners are enjoying their ownership and getting their full value from it.

CHAPTER 8

The Role of Exchange Companies

After working through this chapter, you should be able to understand

- the history of the exchange company.
- the service offers for the vacation owner through the exchange company network.
- the service offers for the vacation ownership developer.

INTRODUCTION

As the timeshare industry began to grow, exchange companies were created to meet the demand of this dynamic market. As more and more people purchased weeks of timeshare ownership, the concept of exchanging weeks was created, providing flexibility to the owners. The basic concept of exchanging one unit for another at a different resort has evolved into many more possibilities (from cruise vacations to weekend getaways) for the timeshare owner, and has thus made vacation ownership even more attractive.

The two largest exchange companies continue to be Resort Condominiums International and Interval International although there are smaller companies that continue to enter the market and offer different types of services, such as contracted management services for resorts, which the larger companies do not offer. This chapter will explore the role of the exchange company focusing on the history and expansion of this segment.

Timeshare Management

HISTORY OF THE EXCHANGE COMPANIES

In 1974, the world's first vacation exchange company, Resort Condominiums International (RCI), was created by Jon and Christel DeHaan. The RCI currently has more than three million members worldwide and over 3700 affiliated resorts. Interval International (II) was formed in 1976. It currently has more than 1.8 million members worldwide and has more than 2000 affiliated resorts. In the mid-1980s, independent exchange companies emerged. It is estimated that although 94 per cent of resorts are affiliated with one or both of the major exchange companies, approximately 9.9 per cent administer their own internal exchange program and 4.9 per cent use other, unspecified exchange services. Tables 8.1 and 8.2 include timelines of both RCI and II to give a picture of how the maturation of the timeshare industry has mirrored the development of exchange companies.

RESORT CONDOMINIUMS INTERNATIONAL

RCI is a global provider of leisure travel services to businesses and consumers, and is the worldwide leader in vacation exchange. This company was created in 1974 as an exchange service for condominium owners and has evolved to meet the demands of a thriving vacation ownership industry. RCI's core business is Exchange Vacations. RCI provides its global community of more than three million timeshare owners worldwide with quality vacation experiences at more than 3700 resorts in 101 countries through RCI's week-for-week and point-based timeshare exchange networks.

The company also offers other services and programs:

The registry collection

This is an international provider of services to the luxury leisure real estate industry with core competencies in exchange service, club operations, travel networks, concierge service, proprietary technology and quality assurance.

Private label clubs

The RCI has helped develop and support many of the world's leading vacation ownership clubs, providing back-office support, high-impact marketing assistance, and branding. RCI's vacation club services feature RCI Points or Weeks exchange services, private labeled to exclusively present the brand identity of an affiliate to create a club, or modify an existing one.

Table 8.1 Resort Condominiums International Timeline

1974: RCI incorporates in Virginia; RCI opens office in Park Fletcher, Indianapolis, Ind.; First resort affiliated; 453 members enroled.

1975: First resort directory published; First member newsletter released; 236 exchanges confirmed; Worldwide timeshare sales total 490 million USD.

1975: First office outside US opens in Mexico.

1977: London office opens; Endless Vacation(s) magazine debuts (32 pages); RCI automates exchange; RCI's annual revenue is 1.5 million USD.

1978: First European timeshare conference held in London.

1979: RCI Travel, a full-service travel agency, opens in Indianapolis.

1980: Offices open in Monaco and Australia; Toll-free lines open seven days a week; Red/Blue/White seasons established.

1981: Offices open in Japan and Florida.

1982: Offices open in Argentina and California; RCI confirms 54 038 exchanges; RCI has 682 resort affiliates.

1983: South Africa office opens; RCI makes 'Inc. 500,' a list of the fastest growing, privately owned businesses in the US.

1984: Offices open in France, Colorado, Massachusetts, and Georgia.

1985: 1000th resort affiliates; RCI Perspective (now RCI Ventures(r)), a magazine for the timeshare industry, debuts for RCI affiliates; Worldwide timeshare sales total 1.5 billion USD.

1986: Holiday, RCI's European member magazine launches; Offices open in Germany and Italy; RCI's headquarters moves to office at Woodview Trace in Indianapolis.

1987: Portugal office opens; RCI confirms 300 000 exchanges.

1988: Offices open in Denmark and Mexico.

1989: RCI has one million subscribing member families; RCI upgrades to IBM's largest computer system, the 3090-400E; RCI's annual revenue is 107 million USD.

1990: RCI adds offices in Venezuela, Greece, Spain, Tenerife and Mexico; RCI handles three million phone calls; Timeshare industry is growing at 15 per cent annually.

1991: Offices open in Canada, and Finland; RCI Gold Crown Resort(r) quality award recognition program established; Disney Vacation Club affiliates with RCI.

1992: Offices open in Singapore, India, and Brazil; RCI confirms 1.14 million exchanges; Resorts of International Distinction resort quality award program established.

1993: Office opens in Turkey; Hilton Grand Vacation Club affiliates with RCI; RCI establishes RCI Management.

1994: Offices open in Egypt and Israel; RCI celebrates 20 years of great vacations with 1.8 million members, 2853 resorts, and confirmations of 1 396 785 exchanges; RCI has 3400 employees at 54 offices in 26 countries.

1995: RCI has two million member families; RCI buys Resort Computer Corp.; RCI opens RCI Consulting.

1996: Office opens in Russia; HFS (now Cendant) purchases RCI; RCI's annual revenue exceeds 300 million USD; RCI.com is launched.

1997: RCI introduces the Preferred Alliances program; RCI affiliates 500th Gold Crown Resort; HFS and CUC International, Inc., merge to form Cendant Corporation, parent company of RCI.

(continued)

Table 8.1   Resort Condominiums International Timeline—cont'd

1998: Vacation Plaza office opens in Indianapolis; Cork, Ireland call centre opens; RCI has 2.5 million members and nearly 3500 resorts.

1999: RCI confirms more than 2.7 million exchanges, sending an estimated 7.5 million people on vacation; RCI world headquarters moves to Parsippany, NJ.

2000: Ken May is appointed Chairman and Chief Executive Officer of RCI; RCI launches the world's first global point-based exchange system, RCI Points.

2001: RCI introduces an exchange program for owners at private residence clubs; RCI establishes a representative office in Beijing, China.

2002: RCI launches a new website for members known as the RCI Community; In the face of a post 9/11 travel slump, US timeshare sales grow by 14 per cent to 5.5 billion USD, further demonstrating traditional resiliency of timeshares ; RCI acquires Hotel Dynamics, a leading provider of occupancy and revenue solutions to hospitality companies; RCI enters the vacation rental market with Holiday Network SM, a worldwide vacation rental channel for consumers; RCI surpasses the three million member mark.

2003: RCI Points has 350 000 members; RCI opens new office in Dubai, UAE; RCI has 3750 affiliated resorts located in 100 countries.

2004: RCI celebrates 30 years of great vacations!

2005: RCI and the Cendant Vacation Rental Group (VRG) operate in a new organization called Vacation Network Group (VNG) headed by Ken May, chairman & CEO. VNG becomes the global leader in leisure accommodations with exclusive access to 55 000 vacation properties worldwide; Cendant announces the breakup of the organization into four separate, publicly traded companies. VNG joins Cendant's Hospitality Group, which includes brands such as Wyndham, Ramada, Howard Johnson, Days Inn and Fairfield Resorts, to form a new company and become one of the world's largest hospitality organizations.

2006: To further leverage RCI's unique brand equity in the timeshare exchange businesses, and in recognition of the recent integration of RCI with European vacation rental businesses, Cendant Vacation Network Group becomes RCI Global Vacation Network; Its Leisure Real Estate Solutions business is renamed NorthCourse; It is announced that Wyndham Worldwide will become the name of the new hospitality company created by Cendant Corporation (NYSE: CD) in the previously announced spin-off of its lodging, vacation exchange and rental, and timeshare resorts businesses; Wyndham Worldwide becomes a publicly traded company on the NYSE under the ticker symbol WYN.

Resort condominiums international public relation material (2007)

NorthCourse leisure real estate solutions

This is the global consultancy and turnkey solutions arm of Group RCI. NorthCourse provides a full spectrum of business advisory and management services, from market research and feasibility studies to full turnkey project management of mixed use and shared ownership real estate developments as well as worldwide sales and marketing solutions.

Hotel dynamics

This is a hospitality services company specializing in the design, evaluation, implementation and management of tailored local marketing programs for the hospitality industry. Today, Hotel Dynamics operates in Africa, Australia, Asia, Europe, Mexico, the Middle East and South America.

RCI weeks and points

RCI Weeks is RCI's traditional exchange system. Vacation exchange adds flexibility and variety to vacation ownership by allowing timeshare owners to trade their Vacation Week for another similar unit. RCI's database of over 3700 resorts in nearly 100 countries enables exchanges to and from resorts around the world. Whether you are interested in domestic or international exchanges, internal exchanges to your home resort, or cruise exchanges, there are thousands of vacation opportunities with RCI.

To exchange, you can:

- **Deposit** – Deposit your Vacation Week into the RCI SPACEBANK® system depository. Your Week is added to the pool of Weeks deposited by RCI Week Members around the world.

- **Request** – Request your Vacation Week Exchange at a comparable resort or resort area for the Week you deposited.

- **Confirm** – Receive a confirmed exchange (the week that is deposited does not have to be taken by another owner before a confirmation is made). If one of your desired resort choices is available, your RCI Guide can confirm your RCI Guide exchange immediately. If a resort unit is not available to fulfill your request, your RCI Guide can enter a computerized search for your desired resorts and travel times and find alternate solutions.

RCI Points is RCI's global point-based vacation exchange system. When a vacation owner joins RCI Points, they will have the flexibility to customize the vacation that is perfect for the owner. RCI Points members are automatically RCI Weeks subscribing members, with complete access to the RCI Weeks system of more than 3700 resorts worldwide. Plus, with RCI's Points

Partner program, the owner can enjoy other leisure prospects such as airline tickets, cruises, hotel stays and other travel- related opportunities.

HOW DO RCI POINTS WORK?

A vacation owner's week is assigned an **RCI Points** value, which simplifies the exchange process. The **RCI Points** value depends on certain factors including the supply and demand at that resort location, the type of unit, season, and evaluations from Members who've stayed there. Your **RCI Points** are made available to the vacation owner annually, at the beginning of your Use Year.

RCI points provides the flexibility to

- choose how many days the owner wants to stay and where the owner wants to
- stay
- vacation at the owner's home resort
- stay at other RCI Points resorts
- reserve a variety of resort unit types and seasons
- save or borrow Points to create vacations
- use RCI Points to book airline tickets, hotel stays, rent a car or book cruises, and
- more offers through RCI's Points Partner Program
- use RCI Points at RCI Weeks resorts

INTERVAL INTERNATIONAL

II which was founded in 1976 does not own or operate resorts, but affiliates them into its global network. Today, that network includes more than 2000 resorts located in over 75 countries and more than 1.7 million member families. II is part of IAC/InterActiveCorp, which operates diversified businesses in sectors being transformed by the Internet, online and offline.

Similar to RCI, II serves both the vacation owner and the developer in a variety of capacities. The vacation owner has the following options for services as members of II:

- **Vacation exchange:** trade your resort week for a world of vacation options.

- **Getaways:** low-priced resort accommodations without exchanging a resort week.

- **Interval Gold:** is the upgraded membership option that offers more year-round discounts, Gold concierge service, and Getaway discounts.

- **Guest certificates:** share the benefits of resort vacation opportunities with friends and families by purchasing a Guest Certificate for exchange accommodations – also available for Getaways.

- **Interval travel:** purchase cruises, airline tickets, car rentals, hotels, and more. Many of the rates are unavailable to the general public.

- **Travel discounts:** receive discounts on car rentals, cruises, and vacation packages.

- **Interval World Magazine:** members-only magazine featuring the latest exchange destinations, member benefits, and travel offers, including getaways and cruises.

II also offers a range of services for the developer. To be competitive, exchange companies have widened the services offered for both developers and owners. The services offered to the developer range from research to financial services and are included in the following section.

Consulting, research and strategic partnerships

II offers developers insights into how to best position their product or develop a resort that meets the current market profile of the vacation owner. They offer these services based on their ongoing research partnerships and offer the developer the following services and information:

- Consumer, development and industry based research

- Business planning

- Strategy development

- Cash-flow modelling

- Feasibility studies

- Competitive analyses

- Market positioning

Table 8.2	Interval International Timeline

1976: II is founded with three employees, one resort, and shoeboxes of index cards.

1977: Interval has now affiliated 60 resorts. There are 10 000 members.

1978: Consumer membership triples to 30 000, with 130 new member resorts.

1980: An IBM computer system and toll-free telephone lines are installed. Consumer membership increases to 80 000, with 250 resorts.

1981: To serve the extensive travel needs of the growing member base, Interval World Travel, known today as Interval Travel, is established.

1982: The II Five Star Award, the industry's first quality recognition program, is created.

1984: Member resort number 500 is affiliated, and Inc. magazine selects Interval as one of the fastest-growing companies in the United States.

1985: Consumer membership increases to 225 000. Interval and Cornell University's School of Hotel Administration develop an exclusive Quality Rating System, and a refined version is still used to measure and maintain the excellence of Interval's resort network.

1987: II introduces WorldCard Preferred, the predecessor of today's Interval Gold and becomes the first in the exchange industry to offer an enhanced membership program.

1988: Dual Exchange, with the Deposit First and Request First methods of vacation exchange, is successfully implemented, giving members more options and flexibility.

1989: Interval begins an ongoing major expansion that will continue for years to come, opening offices throughout Europe, Asia, and Latin America, to best serve consumer members and resort clients.

1991: Interval launched as Worldex Travel Club (now Leisure Time Passport) the industry's first product for non-buyers.

1993: Craig M. Nash, president (now chairman and chief executive officer) of II, receives the American Development Association's (ARDA's) Resort Industry Executive of the Year Award.

1995: By the time, several major hospitality brands and leading independent developers have signed on. II becomes the first vacation exchange company to establish their presence on the Internet.

1996: II celebrates its twentieth anniversary and creates the first Resort Directory on CD-ROM. Membership is now approaching 750 000.

1997: Interval Resort and Financial Services (IRFS) is created as an affiliated company of II, expanding Interval's extensive services to resort developers.

1998: ARDA bestows a Leader of the Year Award on Craig M. Nash.

1999: Interval welcomes its millionth member. Interval Preferred members can take to the seas with the exciting new Cruise Exchange service, and all members can now book Getaways online.

2000: II introduces online, real-time services for booking air travel, hotel reservations, and car rentals.

2001: II celebrates 25 years of exemplary service. Depositing a week, requesting an exchange, and checking on the status of an exchange become as simple as the click of a mouse for members, when Interval launches online exchange.

2002: II is purchased by USA Interactive, the world's leading interactive commerce company, now known as IAC/InterActiveCorp. Interval Preferred relaunches as Interval Gold, which introduces Interval Options, an expansion of Cruise Exchange that includes golf and spa vacations, and the Gold Concierge personal assistant service.

2003: Interval's consumer membership exceeds 1.5 million families, and its global network includes more than 2000 affiliated resorts.

2005: Interval relaunches its member website, IntervalWorld.com, with enhanced functionality.

2006: Nearly 1.8 million families around the globe now enjoy Interval membership 2200 + affiliated resorts in 79 countries.

Source: Interval international public relation material (2007).

Sales support

II provides other services that support the developer in their sales from promotional videos to marketing displays on for their floors to extending options to increase opportunities for potential members and current members of II through the Interval Gold, Leisure Time Passport, and Vacation Certificate program.

Interval gold

Interval Gold, an upgraded membership, offers the following:

- An additional discount off the price of Getaways
- Hertz #1 Gold membership for expedited service in more than 40 airports worldwide
- Entertainment discounts at thousands of selected restaurants, hotels, and stores
- Gold Concierge for the services of a personal assistant, for tasks from the everyday to the extraordinary
- Airline discounts on qualifying flights
- Interval Options, which allows members to trade resort time towards the purchase of a cruise, a golf package, or a spa vacation

Leisure time passport

Leisure Time Passport is a temporary II membership that developers can offer guests that do not make any purchase during their first tour. Developers can package Leisure Time Passport membership with a return stay at their resort, inviting prospects back, or include a certificate for an II-provided vacation.

Vacation certificates

Interval's vacation certificate programs make seasonal over-supplies of resort weeks available to developers as low-cost marketing premiums, first-day incentives and trial-program enhancements with a high perceived value. These weeks both reward prospects and give them firsthand knowledge of vacation ownership.

Interval resort & financial services (IRFS)

Based on the developer's need, II has the following resort and financial services for expediting these vital functions:

- Provides a full range of customized back-office services as an extension of your management operation

- Customized programming of rules of use and fee structures

- Maintenance fee invoicing and collections

- Trial member program servicing

- Processing owner additional night rentals, points transactions, banking, borrowing, etc.

Operational services

II offers back of the house services that aid the smaller developer in providing an affiliation for purchasing for all their in-room housekeeping re-supply needs. Interval Purchasing Services offers more than 10 000 items for over 23 different categories of products including personal care amenities, room accessories, housekeeping supplies, paper products, textiles, and Furniture, Fixtures and Equipment (FF & E).

Professional development

On-site sales and operations training

II representatives will provide on-site training for your sales and operations staff on how to present the II membership benefits to prospective purchasers, and how to provide outstanding service to owners. At each training session, the resort staff will receive a complimentary array of sample membership materials.

VIP club

Interval offers member resorts the Vacation Industry Professionals (VIP) Club, which provides an attractive perk that allows resort employees to purchase weekly Getaway accommodations at reduced prices, and gain a better appreciation of the variety and quality of the resorts in Interval's network.

VIP gold

Affiliates who use the Interval Gold® program can extend this enhanced VIP membership to their employees. Similar to Interval Gold, excluding the exchange feature and Interval Options® VIP Gold allows members to take an additional discount off the already low price of Getaways, enjoy the Gold Concierge service, get discounts on hotels and dining, and receive cash-back on selected travel.

Homeowner's association support

II supports homeowners' associations (HOAs) with the tools they need to stay informed about the company, the industry, and the consumer. The communication program includes the following:

- Customer Satisfaction Index (sent to the HOA president and resort manager)

- Interval's consumer and trade publications: Interval World® magazine, Go IntervalWorld.com newsletter, and Vacation Industry Review

- Complimentary Interval memberships for the HOA Board of Directors

Exchange access system

Interval provides a convenient means of communication with our affiliated resorts via the Internet. EASy (Exchange Access System) links resorts directly with Interval's exchange system. Resort staff can do the following:

- Review and verify ownership details (resort, week, unit, etc.) and make appropriate changes

- View inbound guest information, and owner relinquishing information

- Enroll and/or renew memberships

- Verify and release owners' deposits

- Make corrections and updates to names, addresses and telephone numbers

- Review the Resort Profile and provide changes to Resort Assistance

IRFS single-call servicing

IRFS, an affiliated company of II, offers turnkey reservation services that reinforce the resort's brand and enhance customer service. IRFS provides a full range of back-office services, including single-call servicing, customized with the developer's own greeting. With this program, the resort owners enjoy convenient one-stop shopping for

- Home-resort and club reservations fulfillment

- Interval and external resort exchanges

- Related travel services
- Maintenance fee collection
- Ongoing owner education

Key learning point 8.1

Exchange companies have expanded their service offers to keep up with the rapidly expanding vacation ownership industry. Exchange companies that once only offered simple exchanges to owners now provide a myriad of services that meet the needs of an increasingly demanding market and ownership services to a rapidly growing pool of developers.

CASE STUDY

Jenks Development Company has just purchased a 500-unit condominium complex located in a prime beach location in South Florida. They have been impressed with the growth of the vacation ownership industry and are planning to build purpose-built vacation ownership properties around the world if this venture is successful.

Jenks Development Company has been in business for years, so their main need is to understand the unique aspects of the vacation ownership industry. The company already has a management company that they hope will take over management of the property once all weeks have been sold, so their main concern is find an exchange company that will assist them in business planning and sales and marketing.

The condominium complex is in need of a major renovation to be successful as a vacation ownership property. The company wants to make certain that they have all of the relevant information that they will need to go to a bank so that they will get a competitive loan to pay for the renovation of the project.

Reflective practice

1. Read the case study and find all of the services that are offered by II and RCI that will assist Jenks Development Company with their project.
2. If you were to work as a project manager for Jenks Development Company, what other questions would you have before deciding what company to choose as the properties exchange company?

BOUTIQUE EXCHANGE COMPANIES

There are several smaller exchange companies some of which that are new to the vacation ownership industry and some that have been in business just as long as II and RCI. They are unique in that they fill a smaller, specific niche. The companies that will be discussed in the following section include Trading Places International, Dial an Exchange, and ICE (International Cruise & Excursions, Inc.).

Trading places international

Trading Places began as a full-service travel agency in Southern California in 1973. The company's introduction into vacation ownership began in 1975 when it coordinated 'fly/buy' programs with developers in Hawaii. The first exchange program was developed for a resort in Mexico and the first Trading Places satellite office opening in Hawaii in 1985. In 1994, the company expanded to offer resort management services, and in 1997, the company added timeshare business development offers.

Trading Places International (TPI) is an independent California corporation that offers services to vacation interval owners, resort associations, and resort developers. The company currently ranks third worldwide in independent vacation exchanges confirmed annually. The company does not charge any membership fees but does charge for each exchange that is made. The company also acts as a property manager for some properties which is a service II and RC I do not provide.

TPI has found that 80 per cent of the vacation owners want to exchange to 20 per cent of the vacation destinations; therefore, they focus on high demand regions for exchanges. The company offers the following services:

- Manages owners associations and resorts in Hawaii, mainland US, and Mexico.

- Markets rentals that contribute millions of dollars annually to resorts and vacation owners.

- Operates one of the largest travel agencies based in Southern California offering full-service travel and a cruise agency. The staff is professionally trained and uses systems integrated with timeshare software to offer consumers a 'one-stop shopping' experience.

- Operates on-site Exchange & Travel satellite offices at resorts in California, Hawaii, Nevada and Mexico.

- Offers owner resale programs.

Dial an exchange

Dial an Exchange has the same trading policy as Trading Places International in that they do not have a membership fee and only charge per exchange. The company began operations in Australia in 1995 and extended to Europe in 1999; its mission is to work for the individual timeshare owner and the individual property owner.

Dial an Exchange offers a bank of weeks in vacation properties. Members are given the opportunity to deposit weeks into the bank when they do not wish to use their week. For their deposited week, they receive a credit valid for three years which may be used to withdraw a week out of the dial an exchange system. They may use the week themselves or give it to family or friends.

Most Dial an Exchange members own timeshare apartments; however, an increasing number of owners of managed vacation properties (cottages, villas, condos, townhouses, and apartments) have been using Dial an Exchange Services. This has expanded the variety and number of destinations that are now available to a service which was originally reserved for timeshare properties.

International cruise and excursions, Inc.

International Cruise and Excursions, Inc. (ICE) was founded in 1996 which is a company that provides cruise vacations and resort and hotel vacations. The founders realized that cruise vacations was a missing component to vacation ownership and looked to filling the void. ICE first attained an agreement with Carnival Cruise Lines, then Holland America, Costa Cruise Lines, Cunard, Seabourn and Windstar followed. The company then formed business alliances with resort developers in the United States, Mexico, and the Caribbean.

Membership with ICE provides the vacation owner access to discounted cruise vacations, discounted resort weeks, and land and sea packages. An annual membership fee is required, and some fees are required to use some of the services. ICE is affiliated with more than 650 luxury resort properties and provides cruise and vacation fulfillment services to more than 150 major brands, servicing 55 million consumers. Headquartered in Phoenix, ICE has 700 employees worldwide.

Key learning point 8.2

The boutique exchange companies have been around since the increase in vacation ownership properties. Companies are continuing to find niche markets that have been untapped to meet the needs of independent developers. As the industry continues to evolve, the consumer and developer profile has broadened making room for a more diverse collection of exchange companies.

CASE STUDY

Duckworth Development Company has been researching the vacation ownership industry and believe now is a good time to enter into this segment. They are a small company with no resort management expertise. They have been focusing on Hawaii where they see a great deal of growth potential.

The company had been hesitant to build because of the increase in construction costs but did the math and found out if they build the same property and sell it as a vacation ownership resort, they would be able to use the pre-construction sales proceeds to assist in financing the building of the resort.

Duckworth Development Company considers their expertise in land development and are looking for a company that will provide them with vacation ownership business development expertise before and during development, serve as an exchange company after the property is developed, manage the property and provide association management once the property is ready for opening.

Reflective practice

1. Read the case study and determine what exchange company would be the best match for providing the services that Duckworth Development Company requires for their project.

2. Why do you think an exchange company that offers services other than exchanges helps developers that are inexperienced in the vacation ownership industry?

3. If you were trying to convince Duckworth Development Company to affiliate with your exchange company (a smaller boutique company), what are the key areas that you would believe would assure the company that you would meet their needs?

SUMMARY

Exchange companies have come a long way since the 1970s. From a simple week exchange to fulfilling all of one's travel needs beyond the week that was purchased has created an entrepreneurial environment where nothing is impossible in this constantly evolving business. The symbiotic relationship of increasing the services offered to both the developer and the vacation owner has helped change the definition of vacation ownership. As other competitors enter the market, the standards have heightened, improving the experience for both developers and vacation owners.

CHAPTER 9

Financing in the Timeshare Industry

After working through this chapter, you should be able to

- identify the types of financing used to construct a timeshare

- understand why the timeshare business makes a great deal of money in consumer financing

- understand why consumers choose to purchase a timeshare based on financial reasoning

INTRODUCTION

The timeshare industry has grown because of its ability to bring in funds from different sources (investors, sales of units, revenue generated on site, and consumer financing). This chapter will explain financing from both the developers' and consumers' perspective because comprehension of both parties will assist in seeing why the industry has grown so much during the past 20 years.

The timeshare business model of revenue generated by timeshare resorts consists of three primary components: developing and selling timeshare interests (weeks/points), financing interval interests (weeks/points), and resort management (revenue generated on site via food and beverage, rental of units, etc.). The sales and marketing of the timeshare product consumes a large per cent of the money generated from the timeshare sale. Estimates reported by branded vacation ownership companies indicate that 36–47 per cent of the proceeds of each sale go to sales and marketing costs. This

CONTENTS

percentage is even higher amongst independent non-branded companies. The product cost reported by branded vacation ownership companies resulted in 27–40 per cent of each sale leaving 17–32 per cent for profit and operational expenses (Merrill Lynch, 2007).

Due to the high cost of sales and marketing associated with the timeshare industry, the capital gained by financing the timeshare purchase by the consumer is an integral part of the profit base. Fifty per cent to as high as 70 per cent of timeshare owners finance their purchase through the timeshare resort developer. These loans are usually 12–13 per cent annual percentage interest rate with no pre-payment penalty (Merrill Lynch, 2007).

The timeshare resort developer has the opportunity to go to a bank and acquire a lower interest loan using the timeshare owner's loan to pay for the timeshare week/points as collateral. This type of loan is referred to as an end loan. For example, if the timeshare resort developer charges an owner 14 per cent annual percentage interest rate and they go to a bank and have an arrangement for a 7 per cent annual percentage interest rate for every timeshare owner loan they bring in they will receive 7 per cent profit from the loan. This differentiation between the rate paid by the timeshare owner to the timeshare resort developer and the rate the bank gives the timeshare resort developer is called the spread. The spread generates a continuous cash flow that gives the timeshare resort developer access to funds (in cases of a pre-construction sale) by consumers before the property is built.

Timeshare resorts are also assured a steady stream of funds through the maintenance fees collected by the owners. The average maintenance fee is $555 a week or points equivalent to a week. This assurance of funds helps resort operations in budgetary planning. Timeshare resorts also receive money from food and beverage operations, recreational facilities, and rental of vacant units.

> **Key learning point 9.1**
> Timeshare resort operations receive funding from three different sources: the sale of timeshare weeks, the financing of timeshare weeks, and the collection of funds through maintenance fees and resort operations.

DEVELOPER FINANCING

The unique part of the timeshare industry is that based on the constant flow of income resorts are built quicker than in traditional lodging. The development of timeshare resorts is a complex process requiring different types of financing to complete a project. This next section will include the types of financing a timeshare developer would encounter during the process.

A timeshare developer does not require any financing if they can pay for the project without needing outside financial help. Based on the enormity of the project, this is rarely the case. A developer may need just one of the financing options or all of the options depending on their financial need.

Equity financing

The first type of financing is Equity financing. This is the start-up money needed to begin the project. Office space for the company, salaries of administrative help, hiring of consultants, and other necessities required for the start-up of a project are included in Equity financing. Because the bank is not likely to get any return on their investment at this point if the project fails, this is the hardest type of financing to acquire. Most projects do not attain Equity financing and use their own money and/or investment capital for the start-up money needed for the project.

Acquisition financing

The second type of financing is Acquisition Financing. This is used to buy undeveloped land. The amount of money that is lent for a piece of land is based on its appraised value. The appraised value is based on the current market value of the property, and the extent of clearing, grading, and utilities that have been developed on the property. The extent of infrastructure around the property has bearing as well. If a piece of property is in the middle of nowhere and there are no paved roads reaching the piece of property, a bank may be less inclined to give a developer an Acquisition loan.

This type of financing is no more than three years in duration, and a high rate of interest is charged. The bank does not want the developer to hold on to the piece of land indefinitely because the longer the developer does nothing with the land, the more likely the developer will do nothing with the land and will not be able to pay the bank back. This is why you may see signs on the side of the road stating ACME hotel coming up soon and never see any development, because the developer never received the next level of financing to continue the project.

If a developer has an Equity loan and gets an Acquisition loan, the latter is used to pay off the Equity loan. Now both the Equity loan and the Acquisition loan are lent as one loan to the developer.

Development financing

Development financing is often packaged in the same loan as the Acquisition loan. It is used to develop a piece of land and prepare it for construction. The development loan pays up to 75 per cent of the money required to develop the land. Development loans are short term as well as usually for a period of three years or less. The development of a timeshare property is completed in phases, so only a part of the land that was purchased with the Acquisition loan may be developed at the beginning of a project. After a unit or building is constructed at a timeshare resort and the building has been sold to timeshare owners, another building is planned and another development loan may be taken out for additional construction.

The Development loan is used to pay for the Acquisition loan if money was lent by a bank for this purpose. Remember that the Acquisition loan was used to pay off the Equity loan if one was taken out as well. At this stage, the timeshare developer is paying the Development loan.

Construction financing

Construction financing underwrites the actually building of the timeshare property. The optional loan is when the Construction loan covers some soft goods (e.g. sales and marketing costs) and hard goods (furniture, fixtures, and equipment). However, banks are very reluctant to give a loan for soft goods because if the project fails, they will have a hard time getting their money back from the money lent for this purpose. If a developer receives money for hard goods, they typically only receive 70–80 per cent of the money needed.

Construction loan repayment is based on a release schedule. The idea is to keep the profit with the developer until a greater share of the timeshare units is sold. There is a predetermined cut-off that the money will be due regardless of the units that have been sold to ensure prompt payment of the loan. The release schedule works in the following way: the more the units sold, the higher the interest rate on the construction loan. For instance, if the developer has 5000 weeks to sell, the interest rate may be 5 per cent on the loan until 1000 weeks are sold and then 6 per cent until 2500 weeks are sold and then 7 per cent until the rest of the weeks are sold.

End loan financing

End Loan financing was mentioned earlier in the chapter as a way for developers to use the loans that are financed by the consumer for their timeshare purchase as collateral to obtain the money for construction. The End Loan concept begins when a consumer chooses to finance their loan through the timeshare resort developer. They make a down payment (10–20 per cent of the cost of the timeshare purchase) and they sign a contract to pay the remainder of the money during an agreed-upon time period.

The typical consumer finance rate that a timeshare resort offers is 14 per cent. Before the sales process begins, the timeshare developer will have an End Loan agreement in place with a bank. The bank agrees to give money to the developer for every loan that the developer finances at a set rate. If the developer finances the timeshare sale at 14 per cent and the End Loan agreement with the bank is 7 per cent, the developer will receive the difference between the two rates as profit. The difference between the amount charged to the consumer by the timeshare resort developer and the amount charged by the bank to the timeshare resort developer is called the spread. The larger the spread, the more the developer profits; therefore, a positive working relationship is essential between the developer and the bank.

The typical End Loan agreement lasts between 12 and 18 months between the bank and the timeshare resort developer. This loan is renewed on an as-needed basis, and the interest rate will increase or decrease based on the quality of the loans that are financed by the timeshare resort developer. The bank will lend from 75 to 90 per cent of each loan that the timeshare resort developer finances for the consumer. Again, the better the quality of the loans financed to the consumer by the timeshare resort developer, the greater the access to funds.

The bank that is financing the End Loans for the timeshare resort developer does have restrictions on the End Loans. The timeshare resort developer cannot lend to anyone that chooses to finance through the developer when dealing with End Loans. The End Loan agreement is arranged at the beginning of the project and includes the following: total amount the banks will advance (regardless of the number of loans financed by the timeshare resort developer), interest that the developer will pay, the time period that the commitment to the bank by the timeshare resort developer will last, fees that the bank will be able to charge (e.g. late fees or pre-payment penalties), the size of each loan package given to the timeshare resort developer at any given time, and conditions under which a loan may be considered (e.g. minimum credit score of consumer allowed, minimum income allowed, and no record of bankruptcies on record).

Timeshare resort developers do not need End Loan Financing if they can afford to build without the external funding. The timeshare resort developers

Key learning point 9.2

There are five different kinds of financing used for acquiring and developing land and constructing a timeshare resort. A developer may require no financing or all of the types of financing to complete their project. A positive working relationship with banks before, during, and after development projects is essential for maximizing profits.

that can afford to do this experience a windfall of funds through their consumer financing. For every owner they finance, they receive the full amount of interest that is paid on the timeshare finance loan agreement.

CASE STUDY

Mara and Matt Servaites inherited a hotel on the beach in Florida this past year. They have been doing their research and discovered that the location of their property would be an ideal location to convert the property over to a timeshare development.

They know that the project will need major renovations to convert the hotel rooms into one and two bedroom timeshare villas. They also know that although they have investors, they will need other income to ensure a successful project.

Reflective practice

1. Read the case study and determine whether they will require equity, acquisition, development, and construction financing.
2. What other financing can the developers use to finance the project?

CONSUMER FINANCING

Based on the fact that the average price of a timeshare interval price is $18 502 (AIF Toolkit, 2008) there is no surprise that at least 70 per cent chose to finance through the timeshare resort developer. However, before consumer financing is discussed, the financial reason for purchasing a timeshare from the consumer side needs to be covered. What makes someone walk into a tour and decide at the end that they want to purchase the timeshare week? It is an emotional purchase, but it is a financial one for some as well. The idea of being able to afford to stay each year in a nice condominium for a vacation is a big draw.

If a person spends an average of $200 a night for a hotel room while on vacation staying at a resort and they spend seven nights on vacation at a resort a year and they plan on vacationing for 30 more years, they will be spending $42 000 on hotel rooms and that does not include the cost of tax on the room and inflation. If someone pays $18 502 for a timeshare and pays $555 a year for maintenance fees and goes on vacations for the next 30 years staying at the timeshare resort, they pay $35 152. This figure does not include inflation rates in the maintenance fees either but it is still a smaller figure.

The decision on which would be the biggest money saver would depend on the person. Some people look at 14 per cent financing and see a great deal because they are already putting their hotel room on their 24 per cent credit card. Some people would rather not put anything on credit and pay everything off each year, but are intrigued that if they purchased the timeshare they could in essence lock in today's lodging prices because they would only have to pay the annual maintenance fee after the initial principal is paid off. The reality is people want the luxury today and are willing to pay for it tomorrow in greater numbers.

Consumer financing process

This is the typical consumer financing process that takes place at resorts daily. After the sale while the owner is still on property if they cannot hand over cash or check for the price they must apply to finance the purchase with the knowledge that if they bring in the payment within 90 days, they pay no interest. The resort determines whether the buyer qualifies for financing based on their credit score. If they qualify the down payment that is due that day by the buyer is 10–20 per cent of the purchase price. On some occasions, the resort may take a lower down payment. The length of the loan agreement, corresponding interest rates, amount of each loan payment, and when each loan payment is due is explained during this process.

Again, the buyer can go to any outlet within 90 days to find a better interest rate and acquire the cash to pay the resort without having to pay any interest. However, today seven out of 10 owners finance through the resort, which elicits the question of why? First, with the decline in housing costs, there is less home equity for a person to use to finance purchases. Second, people may have in mind at the time of the purchase that they will find a better deal but never get around to it. Third, people purchasing timeshares at the average rate may not see it as high as what is typically being charged by the credit card companies.

Key learning point 9.3

Consumer financing is a key money maker in the timeshare resort development business. Not all people that go on timeshare tours will qualify for financing, so it is essential to make certain that the tours are marketed to consumers that will have the ability to make a purchase.

CASE STUDY

Jeff and Michelle Williams were invited on a timeshare tour by an OPC (Offsite Procurement Center) at a rest area on their drive down to Florida. They enjoy vacationing in Florida yearly and thought that they could go on the tour and use the two Disney tickets that were being offered by the timeshare resort as a gift for going on the tour.

The Williams have four children and tend to stay in one hotel room that usually costs $59 a night. Of course, when they went on the tour they found the two-bedroom condominium much more inviting than their current accommodations.

Reflective practice

1. Should the Williams purchase the timeshare – yes or no and why?
2. Do you think, based on what you know, about the Williams, they can afford the timeshare?

SUMMARY

The timeshare industry continues to grow because the lodging industry views it as a way to expand while making a substantial profit. This chapter scratched the surface of the finance aspect of the timeshare industry. Because, it is so involved generally the jobs related to financial management are held by people with degrees and experience in financial management. However, the person working in hospitality operations needs to know how the resorts make their money and why the timeshare resort companies can afford to grow at the rate that they have been growing.

CHAPTER 10

Managing Service Quality in Timeshare Operations

'Everything works, everyone smiles and customers feel values'

After working through this chapter, you should be able to

- identify the key problems in managing service quality in timeshare operations

- critically discuss different approaches to service quality management

- operate a suitable service quality management system

- evaluate service quality and create correction strategies

INTRODUCTION

A major concern for destination managers and timeshare operations is to ensure that visitor experiences at least meet expectations. Customer dissatisfaction occurs when customers feel they are not getting what they expect – equipment does not work, facilities are shabby, or staff do not serve them in a hospitable and friendly way. Customer retention and the attraction of new customers depend on ensuring that customers have a clear idea about what to expect from the timeshare operator, and ensuring that they get it! The aforementioned statement sums up the key issues for operators. That is, operators deliver what they say they will deliver. They will be supplying both products and services, and employee performance is a fundamental element of successful service delivery.

Too many timeshare operators have, in the past, paid too little attention to destination visitors' experiences beyond the sale. Yet every destination is competing for customers. They need to

- either retain existing owners and minimize swapping visits away from the site, or

- attract timeshare owners from other destinations, and

- maximize the footfall in their destination.

Maximizing the footfall each week ensures more spending in the destination's shops, restaurants, bars and other leisure services. Fixed costs remain the same, whatever the number of visitors, maximizing the number of visitors in any one week produces higher profits. Creating customer dissatisfaction produces the reverse effect, fewer timeshare owners visit the site in which they own property, fewer non-owners swap into the destination, and this reduces footfall and profits. In effect, the same level of fixed costs is recouped over lower sales volumes – profits fall!

Herzberg (1966) provides a useful model for understanding customer responses to service experiences. Figure 10.1 lists potential dissatisfiers and satisfiers in timeshare services. Essentially, Herzberg suggests the following motivational states.

- Dissatisfiers are those aspects of the service that cause **dissatisfaction** when they are not as expected or defective.

- However, when timeshare visitors find these are as expected, or even better than expected, they do not cause satisfaction, only **an absence of dissatisfaction**.

- Satisfaction only comes from the satisfier list of emotional experiences largely dependent on the dependence of frontline staff. **Satisfied customers** most likely want to return to the destination (Table 10.1).

Table 10.1	Herzberg's Satisfiers and Dissatisfiers Applied to Timeshare Operations
Dissatisfiers	**Satisfiers**
Own timeshare unit décor	Quality of guest/host transactions
Décor of the resort	Hospitableness of hosts
Quality of equipment in unit	Emotional responses to service
Quality of leisure equipment	Treatment as friends
Landscaping of resort complex	Frontline staff performance
Range of leisure facilities	Empathy
Restaurant and bar choices	Feeling at home away from home
Alternative destination attractions	
Range of properties available	

Timeshare and resort operations managers therefore have to not only ensure that the tangible aspects of the offer meet customer expectations to avoid dissatisfaction, but also most importantly to ensure that the service interactions with all staff are hospitable and friendly, and produce a favourable emotional experience for visitors.

Key learning point 10.1

Timeshare resort operations will be more profitable if they attract greater footfall. Better visitor experiences lead to increased customer satisfaction and increased customer footfall.

CASE STUDY

Harry and Norma were excited by the thought of visiting their timeshare resort for the first time. They had been impressed by the high quality design and layout of the resort and their lodge in particular. The resort developer had clearly invested in ensuring that all the timeshare properties were top of the range and all timeshare properties were designed with taste and fitted out with excellent equipment.

Harry and Norma's decision to purchase their week at the resort was influenced by the very nice young woman on the sales team who made them feel really welcome. They felt they were buying a home away from home. The design and fit of their lodge made them feel comfortable, but they were very impressed by the sense of being regarded as one of the family at the resort. So they approached their first

visit with a sense of visiting old friends or even relatives in a new home.

Harry and Norma arrived at the reception in time for the takeover of the lodge; unfortunately, they were told that the accommodation was still being cleaned and would not be ready for another two hours. Harry reminded the receptionist that their new owner's pack stated that lodges would be available from 4.00 pm. The receptionist did apologize, but in an off-hand manner, telling them that a lot of staff had left the resort and they were short of cleaners to service the accommodation. Harry asked to see the manager, but was told that it was his day off, and that the deputy manager was away on a customer-care course. Harry and Norma were very disappointed and made their way to one of the resorts bars for a pot of tea.

Reflective practice

1. Read the case study and comment on the way Harry and Norma were received.

2. How might they have been treated differently?

3. When the manager returns, how should he deal with Harry and Norma?

4. Knowing there were difficulties in servicing the accommodation, how might the resort management have dealt with the problem before the guests arrived?

TIMESHARE SERVICE QUALITY

Timeshare properties clearly represent tangible aspects of the owner's purchase and experience. The location, surrounding area, leisure facilities, restaurants and bars, as well as the individual room, apartment, lodge, or unit that the owners purchase, are all elements of the tangible product which owners purchase, and contribute to their experiences whilst visiting the resort. However, these are not the only aspects of the experiences.

Resort owners and visitors experience a series of services provided by the resort. Contact by the resort operator before the visit, their reception and treatment during the visit and post visit contact together with the restaurant, bar and leisure services they experience whilst at the resort constitute the service elements of the experiences.

These services can be categorized as follows:

1] services related to timeshare ownership, and

2] hospitality services provided to them as visitors to the resort.

The core features of all services, including all timeshare services, are intangibility, inseparability, variability, and perishablility leaving timeshare resort operators with some difficulties and dilemmas to manage in the delivery of services.

The ***intangible*** elements of services make it difficult for customers to establish the benefits to be gained from a service prior to the purchase. This can only be done as a result of receiving the service.

- It is difficult to measure and define the expectations of customers, service employees, and managers in what the intangible benefits should deliver.

- Successful service delivery frequently depends on customers developing feelings of comfort or belonging that are difficult to generate.

The ***heterogeneity*** of services is also a feature that distinguishes them from typical manufacturing production. Service delivery is frequently variable and difficult to standardize because of the personal nature of the contact between the customer and the service deliverer (the staff member).

- Thus, individuals may well vary in their interpretation of customer needs.

- Elements of human 'chemistry' may interfere with performance; some individuals may be more personally committed to successful service encounters.

- Customer expectations of satisfactory service may well vary and be difficult to predict. Hence, it is difficult to say the service delivery is homogeneous, even where the service is relatively simple.

The third important feature of services is that the production and consumption of the service is **inseparable**. This creates a number of differences with typical manufacturing firms.

- Consumers of the service are themselves participants in the service delivery, say as customers in a restaurant or a bar.

- They interact with the service deliverer, the environment and other consumers.

- Customers are party to the service interaction and will partially shape it; they will have their perceptions of the service encounter shaped through their perceptions of the service environment and the perceptions of fellow customers.

Typically, services are subject to **perishability** because they are temporal. Time in the timeshare unit or seats in restaurants represent capacity for a given period.

- Thus, it is not possible to store up sales and satisfy them at another time.

- Nor can any loss of service output be made up at a later date. In many cases, the service is time specific and once lost is gone forever.

- Hence, the empty hotel bed, or unsold restaurant meal represents revenue never to be regained.

- Hospitality retailer service deliverers are not able to stock-pile services, or make up lost service production through overtime working, or multi-source services to allow for fluctuations in the demand and supply of services.

- Service quality faults cannot easily be reworked and given back to the customer, as might happen with a manufactured product.

- Service demand has to be satisfied as and when it is required, so there is difficulty in planning service delivery to meet service demand.

Finally, most timeshare and hospitality services are supplied to customers who do not 'own' the service as supplied; they cannot take it away or return it if unsatisfactory. Because of the intangibility and perishability features, customers frequently buy the right to a service, or an experience. This creates problems of loyalty and memory, unlike the possessors of a tangible product that is taken back home; timeshare consumers rarely have permanent reminders of the product features or benefits. Repeat purchases will be based on a bundle of memories, experiences and expectations. Individual perceptions and differences become important issues.

The matrix given in Table 10.2 does not include an exhaustive list of product and service tangibles and intangibles for timeshare experiences. It does show however that some aspects of timeshare and hospitality operations are more measurable and capable of monitoring than others. The significance of different features will vary between different types of service operations, and the nature of how the characteristics are defined will also vary. For example, *speed* is one of the tangible aspects of the service provided. Most service operational standards lay down target times that the customer should be waiting to be greeted are the reception desk, or for their meals and drinks to be served.

Service requirements vary according to the service being purchased, a root it is important to communicate and expectation and then ensure that the service experienced meets customer expectations.

■ Guest expectations of service quality become an important definitive feature of service quality when set against experiences of the service.

Table 10.2	The quality characteristics matrix for timeshare characteristics of the experience

	Tangible	Intangible
Nature of product	The resort buildings and facilities	Atmosphere
	The individual property and facilities	Décor and furnishings
	The food and drink product offered in the resort	Feeling
	Serving goods – plates – glasses – cutlery – linen, etc.	Comfort
	Information: menu	Perceived quality
	Process – e.g. credit cards	
The contact service	Actions	Warmth
	Accuracy of communication prior to visit	Feeling at home away from home
	Accommodation preparedness	Feeling valued as guests
	Process	Friendliness
	Speed	Care
	Script	Complaint handling
	Corrective action	Fault correction

Source: Adapted from Lockwood (1996)

- Guests have a basic level of expectations of the service – the minimum they expect. They have a level of expectation about what the service should be like versus what they want.

- Guests also predict what they expect the quality to be like

- Visitors may vary in their expectations; customers with more experience of a service may well have higher expectations than those who have less experience of it.

- Timeshare operators have a role in shaping expectations; advertising and other promotional activities may influence consumer expectations.

- It is important that the service delivered in each unit matches these expectations.

Key point 10.2

Timeshare operators have many management problems because of the nature of service means that some aspects of the customer experiences are difficult to define and standardize, and monitor.

SERVICE QUALITY MANAGEMENT SYSTEMS

Given the difficulties inherent in service delivery, quality management systems have been developed for the quality management services. These have been used extensively in hospitality and timeshare operations. They aim to be a little more responsive to the intangible elements of service but, as we shall see later, are often unable to capture the key transactions between guests and hosts which differentiate hospitality and timeshare services from other services.

SERVQUAL has been widely used by hotel companies to compare customers' expectations with their experiences and thereby show where service delivery has strengths and weaknesses. The performance of different competitors can be compared with the service organization's own performance. In particular, it reveals 'five service gaps' where there may be a mismatch been the expectation of the service level and the perception of the service delivered. Table 10.3 highlights the five dimensions that have been identified for the basis for the SERVQUAL system of quality evaluation.

The model defines the five dimensions of service, and suggests that these provide a framework for understanding where the service quality management problems are occurring. There are some physical elements included under the tangibles, but most of the items included relate to employee performance. Hence, frontline staff recruitment, induction, training and development, motivation, rewards and performance monitoring are crucial elements of the management of service quality (see Chapter 11). Employee performance with customers is a key determinant of service quality delivery and of customer satisfaction.

Service gaps focus on the points at which expectations of service requirements by management, the standards set, the standards achieved, or the service standards communicated to customers produce a situation where customers' perceptions of the **service delivered** do not match with the **expected service**.

Responsiveness, assurance and empathy are elements of this model that underscore the importance of employee performance in the service encounter. Given the nature of services, it is often difficult to predict what employees have to say or do in given service encounters (Table 10.3).

Reflective practice

1. Consider the SERVQUAL service gaps model and show how a timeshare management operator might use it to assess service quality in a timeshare resort.

2. Return to the case study and identify which service gaps were involved in the treatment of Harry and Norma?

3. What actions might the resort manager take to ensure the problems do not persist?

Table 10.3 The five dimensions of service

Dimension	Definition
Reliability	The ability to perform the promised service dependably and accurately
Tangibles	The appearance of physical facilities, equipment, personnel and communication materials
Responsiveness	The willingness to help customers and provide prompt service
Assurance	The knowledge and courtesy of employees and their ability to convey trust and confidence
Empathy	The caring individualized attention paid to the customer

Given the clear importance of employee performance, some writers look to *critical incidents* in which employee responses can be shown to either save a situation and create customer satisfaction or can make a bad situation create dissatisfaction.

Their findings suggested three broad groups of incidents:

- employee responses to service delivery system failures.

- employee reactions to customer needs and requests.

- unprompted and unsolicited employee actions.

Each group represented a cluster of incidents in which employee behaviour could result in customer satisfaction or dissatisfaction (Table 10.4).

Employee responses to service delivery system failures can be critical, because customers are more likely to excuse a service failure if the fault is acknowledged and quickly corrected. Any problem that is not corrected at the

Table 10.4 Positive and negative response to critical service incidents in timeshare operations

Critical incident	Customer satisfaction	Customer dissatisfaction
Employee responses to service delivery failure	Could be turned into incidents which employees use to advantage and generate customer satisfaction. If an employee reacts quickly to service failure by responding sensitively to customer experiences, say by compensating the customer or upgrading a customer to a higher status service.	More frequently, however, staff responses were likely to be a source of dissatisfaction – where the employee fails to provide an apology, an adequate explanation or argues with the customer
Employee responses to customer needs and requests	Employee responsiveness, flexibility and confidence that they can match whatever is needed by the customer are important sources of a positive customer response.	Similarly, employee intransigence, inflexibility, and perceived incompetence are all likely sources of customer dissatisfaction.
Unprompted and unsolicited employee actions	This might involve employee behaviours which made the employee feel special, or where an act of unexpected generosity took the customer by surprise.	Customer dissatisfaction could be the result of a failure to give the customer the level of attention expected, or inadequate information, or might involve inappropriate behaviour such as the use of bad language, etc.

unit may result in complaints to the head office, and more importantly a lost customer. Taking into account that each customer tells friends and relatives, the lost customer can cost far in excess of the replaced meal or free bottle of wine.

Similarly, employee reactions to customer needs and requests are important in all service situations because there are bound to be occasions when customers want something that is not normally sold via the brand, or where they make a mistake and want some assistance in correcting their fault. Customers are much more likely to respond positively if they are treated with flexibility and the service employee makes every effort to meet their needs.

Unprompted and unsolicited employee actions incorporated actions which were outside of the customer's expectations of the service encounter. Where employee performance is beyond the customer's expectation of the service, the incident can produce satisfaction – exceeding customer expectations may involve the details of their performance. Employees in TGI Fridays are encouraged to perform in a way that underpins the brand's offer to customers that involves humour and a 'fun' atmosphere. This often involves providing balloons or singing songs at a birthday celebration.

The issue of employee performance and customer satisfaction takes on added urgency when firms begin to consider the costs of lost business and the benefits of generating customer loyalty.

Reflective practice

1. Using the case study, suggest how the receptionist might have responded to the customers' satisfaction.
2. What do you think were Harry and Norma's expectations?
3. What actions by the receptionist might have exceeded Harry and Norma's expectations?

Key point 10.3

Service quality management systems suggest that frontline employee performance is key to delivering quality service experiences for timeshare resort visitors.

QUALITY MANAGEMENT AND TIMESHARE OPERATIONS

The earliest developments in quality stem from the manufacturing industry and timeshare organizations have adopted and adapted these different approaches, though these different systems do not always match the needs of the organization, and different organizations need to adapt the system to their offer to customers. The following provides a brief overview of different systems and terms used

Quality inspection	■ Actual output of a product or service is checked against a standard specification. Defects are then reworked or sent for scrap. Whilst quality inspection is undertaken via line managers – quality inspectors and mystery customers, the approach is frequently limited by the nature of the timeshare products and services. It is not always possible to rework a faulty product or service. Also there is no way of identifying the cause of the fault. ■ However, this system will be used widely by timeshare resort developers when completing the construction of physical buildings and facilities.
Quality control	■ Quality is designed into the detailed specification in the manufacture of products and services through detailed standards. Quality checks are introduced through the various stages of the process, say between departments. At root, the approach is still concerned with the detecting and correcting of faults. It will not improve in quality, but it does show when quality is not present. ■ The use of mystery customers has been used widely in resort and timeshare operations management. The mystery customer acts as a customer and makes a report on the experience to management. ■ Again the quality control process of checking and fault detection is built into the process used by many resort developers
Quality assurance	■ Rather than waiting for faults to occur, quality is designed into the process in a way that faults cannot occur. If faults do occur, they are corrected as they happen. The approach involves developing a documented and planned quality system. Quality assurance requires total organization commitment and involvement of all employees in the process. A key problem is that although quality assurance may consistently deliver faultless products and services, it may not be what customers want.
Total quality management	■ The focus is on customers and the satisfaction of customer needs. The system is totally directed at customer satisfaction and the removal of any barriers to delivering customer satisfaction. People in the organization are key to successfully achieving customer satisfaction – employee training, motivation and empowerment are important. Again successful implementation needs total cultural commitment and this can be difficult, because it is often hard to change the organization's culture. ■ This provides a potentially valuable model for successful service quality delivery in resort management.

The approaches listed above are not by themselves mutually exclusive; one approach builds on another and effective quality programmes often incorporate aspects of all these approaches. So systems based on Total Quality Management still need to involve quality inspection and quality control, though the number of faults and problems should be greatly reduced.

Key point 10.4

Service quality management systems are most effective if they are able to prevent service failures in the first place.

Reflective practice

1. Consider the four types of quality management and identify the potential causes of the problem faced by Harry and Norma.

2. Which of the approaches are most likely to prevent the same sort of problem from happening again?

TOTAL QUALITY UNIT MANAGEMENT

Resort managers may be working within an organization that employs one or the other of the systems discussed; in some cases there may be no formal system for defining, managing and monitoring service quality in the time-share. Total Quality Management provides a useful model that can be employed across the whole organization, or in the individual resort.

■ Timeshare resort organizations require quality systems that are holistic enough to allow for the characteristics of services and the varied perceptions of customers. TQM appeared to offer service organizations the required system.

Even though there are several forms of Total Quality Management, the following list of principles covers several broad features of TQM which are found in most descriptions of the initiative.

■ At heart, the initiative locates a commitment to quality services as a core organizational concern. The commitment of senior management is crucial and the approach has to permeate every aspect of the organization.

- The approach has been particularly attractive to timeshare resort operations because it aims to create a cultural environment in which employees, operating independently, are guided by a commitment to delighting customers because they have internalized the organization's objectives and values.

- These internalized values, beliefs and objectives ensure that employees aspire to achieve customer satisfaction and quality improvement, without extrinsic controls or inducements (Table 10.5).

The similarities between TQM and empowerment are not accidental because many of those writing about the benefits of TQM as an approach for managing service organizations also advocate the need to empower with authority to correct defects and respond to service failures as they occur. Furthermore, employee empowerment is important so that employees can respond to unusual customer requests, or use their experience and creativity to look for ways of delighting the customer. These aspirations for TQM and empowerment are relevant to the three critical incidents that could create, or damage, customer satisfaction:

Table 10.5	Principles of total quality management

1. Highest priority given to quality throughout the organization
2. Quality is defined in terms of customer satisfaction
3. Customers are defined as those who have both internal and external relationships with the organization – includes employees, shareholders, the wider community
4. Customer satisfaction and the building of long-term relationships are at the nub of the organization
5. The organization's aims will be clearly stated and accessible to all
6. The principles, beliefs, values and quality are communicated throughout the organization
7. Total Quality Management creates an ethos which pervades all aspects of the organization's activities
8. Core values of honesty, integrity, trust and openness are essential ingredients of TQM
9. The Total Quality organization is intended to be mutually beneficial to all concerned and operates in a climate of mutual respect for all stakeholders
10. The health and safety of all organization members and customers are given priority
11. Total Quality offers individuals the chance to participate and feel ownership for the success of the enterprise
12. Commitment is generated in individuals and teams through leadership from senior management
13. TQM results in an organization-wide commitment to continuous improvement
14. Performance measurement, assessment and auditing of the organization's activities is a common feature of TQM
15. TQM aims to use resource more effectively and members are encouraged to consider ways of using resources more effectively
16. TQM requires appropriate investment to ensure that planned activity can occur.

- dealing with service failures,

- responding to request for unusual service, and

- providing extraordinary interactions,

are all occasions when employee behaviour impacts either positively or negatively on customer satisfaction and perceptions of service quality. TQM provides an organizational setting in which empowered employees, through a heightened sense of their own personal efficacy, will respond in the desired way.

CASE STUDY

The resort in which Harry and Norma have bought their timeshare property is on the site of a major international hotel in a large estate with two championship quality golf courses.

Before Harry and Norma's visit, a terrorist incident had resulted in a 25 per cent decline in the number of visitors from the hotel's key international market. The Head office had instructed the Hotel General Manager to dismiss 15 per cent of hotel employees, and many others had resigned from the hotel. Cleaning services, bar and restaurant and reception staff had been particularly affected. In fact, earlier in the day before Harry and Norma arrived, the receptionist in question had confided in a friend that she thought she was next in line for dismissal. She was very worried because this was one of the few jobs in the area, and she had a sick mother to look after.

Reflective practice

1. How might the hotel management have behaved differently?

2. What impact did their actions have on Harry and Norma's experience?

3. How would a TQM organization have handled the situation?

Key learning point 10.5

Total Quality Management suggests a management approach which develops a service culture dedicated to prioritizing customer service experiences, and doing whatever it takes to delight customers.

HOSPITABLENESS

The traditional service quality literature suggests that employee performance is a key determinant of service quality, and thereby customer satisfaction. In particular, the intangible aspects of services and the need to provide unique service experiences to customers, together with the perishability of services, mean that service deliverers have a fundamental role to play. That said, timeshare experiences are fundamentally about hospitality and acts of hospitableness.

This chapter argues that these techniques fail to recognize the potentially unique relationship between guests and hosts in timeshare operations. That is not to say that the more conventional and rational approaches do not have a place, but there is a need to recognize that hospitality and tourism experiences have important emotional dimensions that traditional marketing approaches tend to underplay. By understanding the hospitality transaction between guests and hosts, marketers and commercial operators can deliver customer experiences through which to build customer loyalty. Whilst the general service literature is helpful, it fails to see the essential role of providing hospitable experiences for guests.

Extending hospitality to strangers is an ancient tradition stretching back to thousands of years, though many contemporary societies have lost touch with these traditions. Yet, contemporary modern societies can take note of these traditions of hospitality and hospitableness to better understand guests' needs and to build a genuinely competitive advantage. To better understand the commercial applications of hospitality, it is necessary to explore hospitality in its widest sense.

In times past, hospitality and the need to be hospitable were highly valued in all communities. Being genuinely hospitable to travellers and less fortunate members of the community was seen as a good thing and was highly valued. In contemporary modern societies today, hospitality and the expectation to be hospitable are not afforded anything like the same cultural and religious status as was given in the past.

Importantly, being hospitable in a private setting involves the host being responsible for the guest's happiness. There is a special link and the guest is in a mutual pact. The host becomes the guest and the guest becomes the host on another occasion. In private domestic settings, hospitality

- involves mutual giving and obligation,

- includes generosity,

- is about being unselfish,

- is about being open-handed,

- involves welcoming people,

- concerns warmth

Most importantly, hospitality is based on appropriate motives and is more than hosting. A good host may be effective at keeping glasses full, food on the table and the room temperature comfortable, but may have ulterior motives – say to win favours, or for reasons of seduction or vanity. Good hospitality requires the right motives:

- the desire for the guest's company,

- the pleasure of entertaining,

- the desire to please others,

- concerned for the needs of others,

- a duty to be hospitable.

Hospitable people are those who possess one or more of these motives for entertaining. This raises the difficulties faced by many timeshare organizations. The commercial rationale in which they operate often distorts the relationship with their guests. The commercial rationale sells timeshare based hospitality as a commodity. Guests become customers, and both the host and guest develop a reduced sense of mutual obligation. A consequence is that many timeshare organizations report difficulties in retaining customers and want to develop more repeat visits by existing customers.

Clearly, individual timeshare resort operators cannot change society's sense of hospitality nor run their operations as though they were private domestic hosts, but they might be better able to build a community of customers more robustly loyal if they better understood hospitality in these contexts. For example, genuine hospitality is closely linked to values of generosity, beneficence and mutual obligations. Without wishing to suggest that profit driven organizations would be willing to give away their product, consideration of how regular customers can be rewarded with extra benefits which celebrate their importance and uniqueness as individuals could be successful. The key here is to making the giving seem like acts of genuine generosity rather than the formulaic 'give-aways' typical of many branded hospitality businesses.

Timeshare operators also need to consider the recruitment, selection and training of hosts who are capable of being hospitable, and who display characteristics of hospitableness. The implication is that the recruitment of people who genuinely reflect and work to the values of hospitableness, and train to these values is important for building loyal customers.

Reflective practice

1. Think back to different times when you have been a guest in someone's home. Are there differences in the way hosts treat you? Think of good and bad experiences and compare them.

2. Consider occasions when you or your family have acted as hosts. How do you behave with guests? Compare this with your experiences as a guest.

3. In both cases, did you feel obliged to act in certain way?

Key learning point 10.6

Learning from traditional obligations to be hospitable can provide a means for building relationships with customers that create a feeling of being welcomed and wanted. Building emotional ties which are difficult to replicate provides the basis for developing customer loyalty and competitive advantage.

SUMMARY

This chapter has shown that customer service quality management is an important, if not vital, aspect of timeshare resort management. The retention of existing customers, and the attraction of new customers to the resort are essential for sales growth. Certainly the loss of regular customers has a real material impact on sales revenues and profits. In addition, dissatisfied customers rarely keep their experiences to themselves, and by the time they tell friends and acquaintances, the loss in business can run into thousands of pounds.

Service quality management is difficult because customer satisfaction is associated with customer expectations. Not all customers use the resort for the same occasions, and their expectations and assessment of incidents critical to service success vary. In addition, employee assessments of customer needs may also not match the customer expectation. In addition, the nature of the service encounter itself is difficult because of the intangible aspect of service and the difficulties caused by the perishable nature of hospitality and timeshare services. It is not possible to rework a smile or a false greeting.

Given these difficulties, many hospitality and timeshare resort organizations have explored a number of national and international award schemes that both provide a framework for designing and delivering quality and provide a 'kite-mark' for customers and clients. Even in situations where there is no award system, Total Quality Management provides a useful philosophical model for the resort. Different types of service offers will require different TQM approaches, but all depend on a cultural commitment to delivering high-quality service. Also, employee skills and performance are essential to successfully meeting customer expectations.

CHAPTER 11

Human Resources in Timeshare Operations

'People matter so manage as though they do!'

After working through this chapter, you should be able to

- critically discuss the qualities of hospitableness and customer experience

- identify the emotional dimensions of hospitality services

- evaluate the role of employee empowerment in managing customer experiences

- evaluate people management practices required to deliver remarkable customer experiences

CONTENTS

INTRODUCTION

Timeshare service experiences are delivered by frontline staff, and ultimately customer memories and perceptions of the resort will be largely determined by the performance of those serving them. As we saw in Chapter 10, the literature on service quality suggests that customer satisfaction and long term customer loyalty are the result of customer experiences and the extent that these match prior expectations. This chapter argues that, in fact, timeshare experiences are likely to be influenced by the transactions between host and guest and dependent on experiences of hospitality and hospitableness.

145

This chapter recognizes that timeshare operations involve service interactions whereby the nature of the frontline staff performance has a major impact on customer evaluations of service quality (Langhorn, 2004). That said, hospitality operations are different from traditional services because they are linked to the emotional experiences associated on a number of levels with hospitality, and the relationship between guest and host as well as between domestic and commercial dimensions of hospitality (Lashley, 2000; Lashley and Morrison, 2003; Lashley et al., 2004, 2007). Traditional service quality management instruments rarely recognize these strong emotional dimensions of the service interaction in the context of hospitality (Parasuraman et al., 1991), and consequently underplay the importance of the emotional performance of frontline staff and line management for effective performance. Even those who do recognize that it takes 'happy workers to create happy customers' (Barbee and Bott, 1991) fail to recognize the emotional complexities of the host and guest relationship, and rely on the reproduction of a 'Have a Nice Day Culture' (Mann, 1998, 1999).

These emotional demands on both service workers and their managers have implications for the way employees are managed, and for employment practices and techniques.

- Empowerment has the potential to engage employees in delighting customers not only through the quality of their personal performance, but also in developing more emotional harmony.

- Empowered employees are likely to feel more satisfied in their work and not feel the stress arising from emotional disharmony (Mann, 1999).

- Empowerment has the potential to give frontline employees the freedom to meet (or exceed) customer service expectations through the quality of their treatment of guests, as well as improve staff job satisfaction and commitment to the firm and its objectives (Parson, 1995).

Therefore, it is important that the timeshare industry manages its workforce in a way that recognizes the central importance of employee performance.

Key learning point 11.1

Frontline employee performance has a major impact on visitor experiences of the resort and thereby influences levels and extent of visitor returns.

CASE STUDY 11.1

Harry and Norma were excited by the thought of visiting their timeshare resort for the first time. They had been impressed by the high quality design and layout of the resort and their lodge in particular. The resort developer had clearly invested in ensuring that all the timeshare properties were top of the range and that all timeshare properties were designed with taste and fitted out with excellent equipment.

Harry and Norma's decision to purchase their week at the resort was influenced by the very nice young woman on the sales team who made them feel really welcome. They felt they were buying a home away from home. The design and fit of their lodge made them feel comfortable, but they were very impressed by the sense of being regarded as one of the family at the resort. So they approached their first visit with a sense of visiting old friends or even relatives in a new home.

Harry and Norma arrived at the reception in time for the takeover of the lodge; unfortunately, they were told that the accommodation was still being cleaned and would not be ready for another two hours. The Receptionist serving them was very apologetic and said that this was an unusual occurrence, and doubly unfortunate as this was Harry and Norma's first visit. She said that a table had been reserved for them in the restaurant for afternoon tea which was complimentary and they were invited to dine with the Resort General Manager that evening, and again there would be no charge to the guests.

Harry and Norma had a wonderful afternoon tea, they did not eat too much because they wanted to 'save some room for dinner', as Harry commented. Dinner turned out to be a memorable occasion, Harry and Norma were made to feel very special.

After the vacation, Harry and Norma told all their friends what a nice time they had had at the resort, and persuaded several friends to also take out a timeshare week at the resort. In fact, their friends joined Harry and Norma each year, and their holiday at the resort became a regular event.

HOSPITALITY AND HOSPITABLENESS

Recent work exploring the nature of hospitality (Lashley and Morrison, 2000; O'Mahony, 2003; Lashley and Morrison, 2003; Lynch, 2005) and hospitableness (Telfer, 2000) provide insights into the kind of service that customers expect from the tourist and hospitality industries. On one level, hospitality and tourism operations encompass commercial hospitality industry activities, 'the provision of food and/or drink, and/or accommodation in a service context' (HEFCE, 1998). However, hospitality and tourism services also involve a relationship between guest and host which is rooted in cultural, ethical and religious traditions.

- Classic definitions of hospitality suggest that it is a social phenomenon with roots in societies thousands of years ago (O'Gorman, 2005).

- In this context, hospitality has been described as the giving of food and sometimes accommodation to people who are not normally members of the household (Telfer, 2000).

- Traditional hospitality required the host or giver of the hospitality to share these things in their own home, and share their own food and drink with their guest at no charge or fee.

- Hospitality involves hosts sharing their home with strangers and at the same time accepting responsibility for their guests' safety and welfare and happiness.

'If this is a host's task, it is concerned with more than food, drink and shelter: it means that a host must try to cheer up a miserable guest, divert a bored one, care for a sick one' (Telfer, 2000).

- However, the key responsibility of the host is to ensure the safety and the well-being of the guest whilst he or she is on the host's home or premises.

Acts of hospitableness involve being hospitable for genuine motives (Telfer, 2000).

- Typically, these involve the desire to please others, through feelings of friendliness and benevolence or through enjoyment in giving pleasure.

- They may involve feelings of compassion for others or a desire to entertain friends.

- Truly hospitable behaviour has a concern for providing hospitality through helping, entertaining, protecting and serving guests.

- Where there are ulterior motives – being hospitable to win favour or advantage with others, or for reasons of personal vanity – behaviour is not genuinely hospitable.

Traditions of hospitality have a long history with examples predating Christianity. In Ireland, for example, 'In Irish tradition, hospitality was not merely a virtue but an over-riding duty' (Mahon, 1991: 10). Primitive Christians also considered it to be a sacred duty and moral imperative to receive, feed, lodge and protect any traveller who stopped at their door. As a Christian Scholar noted in Ireland,

'Bid they guest welcome, though they should come at every hour. Since every guest is Christ – no trifle saying this; better is humility, better gentleness, better liberality towards the guest.' (Mahon, 1991: 10).

People would be rewarded or punished either on earth or in the after life as a result of how they treated the stranger among them (Pitt-Rivers, 2002).

From a twentieth-century Christian perspective, Nouwen (1975) argues that such hospitality should consist of the following facets:

- Free and friendly space – creating physical, emotional and spiritual space for the stranger

- Stranger becomes a guest – treated as a guest and potential 'friend'

- Guest protected – offer sanctuary to the guest

- Host gives gifts – the host welcomes the guest by providing the best gifts possible

- Guest gives gifts – the guest reciprocates and gives gifts to host

- All guests are important and gifted – the host values the guest and gains value from them

- Acceptance, not hostility – especially the kinds of subtle hostility, which makes fun of strangers or puts them into embarrassing situations

- Compassion – hospitality is basically a sense of compassion

The importance of the emotions of hospitality is reinforced by work on the emotions of 'special meal occasions' (Lashley et al., 2004). Respondents asked to describe their most memorable meal identified the emotional dimensions that make meal occasions, and thereby hospitality, special.

- The occasion of the meal or holiday is often a celebration of bonding and togetherness with family and friends.

- The company of others.

- The atmosphere created by the setting.

- Other people and their treatment by hosts provide emotional dimensions to meal occasions for guests which are vital to creating memorable occasions.

- Interestingly, few of the respondents mentioned the food consumed as part of their descriptions. The dominant impression is that these emotional dimensions of hospitality are what make a meal occasion or a guest's stay in a hotel special.

Respondents in this research used language that links their experiences back to domestic hospitality. The need to feel welcome and the friendliness of hosts, being secure in a non-threatening environment, feeling comfort and warmth were all words used to describe guests' emotions and experiences.

Commercial settings are not always a lesser form of hospitality; they engage guests with some different emotions, but there are some important overlaps. Fundamentally, guests evaluate hospitality experiences primarily in emotional terms and providers of hospitality experiences in hospitality and tourism resorts need to be aware of these emotional dimensions of the customers' experiences and how to meet these emotional needs.

The emotional dimensions of the visitors' experiences are an important consideration for the management of hospitality and tourism operations. Although traditional obligations to be hospitable to strangers began to break down in many countries industrial societies in the nineteenth century (Mahon, 1991), modern tourists clearly perceive traditional hospitality as an important consideration in their decisions to visit the destination. Nine out of 10 overseas visitors claim that friendly and hospitable people were a factor in choosing to visit the country (Fáilte, 2005). Recognizing the importance of these perceptions of traditional hospitality, it is important to understand the emotional dimensions of hospitality and tourism encounters, and the potential impact of management on either enhancing or retarding these emotional dimensions through the management of service employees.

> **Key learning point 11.2**
>
> The obligation to be a good host is not just limited to private domestic settings, nor to past history. Commercial hospitality and timeshare operations can gain a lot from providing genuine hospitality to guests.

EMOTIONAL DIMENSIONS OF HOSPITALITY AND TOURISM SERVICE

Clearly, service operators are generally aware of the importance of having the right kind of emotions on display in service encounters; hence their concern that staff display emotions is appropriate to the service offer (Hochschild, 2003). Usually, this is typified as smiling and the 'Have a Nice Day' culture (Mann, 1999). The problem is that the specific features of the hospitality service interactions relevant to tourism operations are 'more than a service encounter' (Lashley et al., 2004) and the emotional dimensions of performance need to be given a pre-eminence that they rarely receive in performance monitoring and quality management systems.

Furthermore, Hochschild's seminal work (2003) suggests that service workers are prone to provide emotional labour that can add to job stress and which results in burn-out and staff retention problems. Emotional labour is the result of having to display an emotion that individuals do not feel, or the result of the need to mask emotions that are felt but are not deemed to be legitimate for the service encounter; for example, when an employee is required to smile even though angry and upset, or when the employee must restrain his/ her anger when dealing with an awkward and complaining customer. Mann (1998) suggests that there are potentially three emotional states when dealing with customers. Each of the states is created as an interaction between the emotions felt, the emotions displayed and the emotional performance required of the job role.

1. From a service perspective, emotional harmony is the desired state because it requires less emotional labour, it causes less stress and is more acceptable to customers. This is because the emotions expressed are those genuinely felt and required of the job holder. Langhorn's study (2004) of emotional performance and emotional intelligence in a UK popular restaurant chain found that staff who were able to display 'service emotions', which they genuinely felt, were perceived by customers as giving better service, better value and as generating the customers' desire to return to the restaurant.

2. Emotional dissonance and emotional deviance are less desirable. Emotional dissonance is the classic state of emotional labour that has negative effects on employees. Langhorn's study suggests that customers are less impressed with staff performance where the person appears to be acting and are trying to hide emotions felt, particularly where these are negative emotions.

3. Emotional deviance will clearly create a negative customer response, resulting in poor evaluations of the service experience, because the emotions being expressed are not appropriate to the service encounter. Hospitality and tourism operators need to consider these dimensions of the service interaction, and how to support their emotional labourers, who are key to good customer relations and the generation of loyal customers.

The work on emotional labour has stimulated interest in the emotional dimensions of organizational life (Fineman, 1993; 2000). The impact of emotional intelligence has been seen as a key influence on business success in commercial organizations with particular relevance for services. Emotional Intelligence has been described as key to organizational success, with particular relevance in organizations like hospitality and tourism and hospitality services, where employee (internal customer) relations impact so directly on external customer experiences. Goleman puts emotional intelligence at the leading edge of business success. 'The business case is compelling: companies that leverage this advantage [emotional intelligence] add measurably to their bottom line' (Goleman, 1998: 13).

The notion of an Emotional Intelligence Quotient is being widely promoted by many consultants and is said to underpin the most effective business performance and successful lives (Cooper and Sawaf, 1997). Those who are emotionally intelligent are said to have abilities in five domains. They:

1. recognize their own emotions and express them to others

2. recognize and understand the emotions of others

3. use emotions with reason and emotional information in thought

4. regulate and manage their own and the emotions of others

5. control strong emotional states – for example, anger, frustration, excitement, anxiety

Hospitality and tourism operators might be able to improve business performance and customer satisfaction with management practices rooted in emotional intelligence practices. Langhorn (2004) studied the emotional intelligence scores of managers and staff in a popular chain restaurant group in the UK. He found that managers with higher emotional intelligence scores were positively related to improved profit performance, customer satisfaction, employee satisfaction and team performance. Employee emotional intelligence scores were positively linked to customer perceptions of service quality and value, and willingness to return. Improvements can be made in operational performance through recruitment and training practices, as well as performance and service quality monitoring that use emotional intelligence as a key business concern.

The emotional dimensions of hospitality make the relationship between host and guest more than just an ordinary service encounter. Resort visitors are likely to evaluate their total experience on the basis of their various encounters with frontline personnel from all organizations involved in the complete holiday experience and the feelings generated by such encounters. An awareness of these emotional dimensions leads to a concern for the emotional labour undertaken by frontline employees, and the conditions needed both to remove negative impacts and generate emotions that are genuinely hospitable. Recent interest in assessing, recruiting and developing the emotional intelligence of service workers offers one interesting avenue for the improvement of service encounters. Employee empowerment also has the potential to create the conditions that will improve employee service performance by creating the conditions that are likely to result in emotional harmony.

All this confirms the importance of some basic human resource management practices. In the first instance, it is essential that the right people are recruited from the start. Selection and recruitment practices should be carefully defined and planned. Erecting high barriers to entry will ensure that entry to jobs in hospitality and tourism sectors goes beyond breath on the mirror approaches, whereby anyone demonstrating signs of life is deemed employable (Lashley and Rowson, 2000). Careful and considered recruitment is concerned essentially with recruiting the right person with high levels of social skill and emotional intelligence (Langhorn, 2004). Where necessary, the skills are further developed by planned and targeted staff development, and the retention of emotionally intelligent staff is given a high priority by managers who are themselves providing emotional leadership (Lashley, 2004). It has been claimed that emotional harmony can be created with use of empowerment (Lashley, 2001).

> **Key learning point 11.3**
> Emotional dimensions of service help customers feel good or bad about a service encounter. Staff having to provide less than genuine emotional displays can undergo added job stress through the provision of emotional labour.

EMPOWERING SERVICE EXCELLENCE

The problem is that employee empowerment is one of those management terms that sounds good, because of the meaning that empowerment has in everyday language. The Collins English Dictionary (1993: 498) provides two meanings, '1. to give or delegate power or authority to; authorize. 2. to give ability to; enable or permit'. Yet examples of empowerment in practice cover a whole host of different situations, some of which encompass these definitions and others that clearly do not.

Restaurants and hotels often incorporate the idea of empowerment into their employee training schemes and management philosophy.

- In the Accor group of hotels, for example, empowerment has been used to describe the use of 'quality circles';

- In McDonald's Restaurants, suggestion schemes;

- 'Whatever it Takes' employee training programmes in Marriott Hotels; employee involvement in devising departmental service standards in Hilton International Hotels;

- Semi-autonomous work groups and removal of levels of management in Harvester Restaurants; and

- The delegation of greater authority to hotel general managers (Lashley, 2001).

In fact, these examples cover quite different arrangements in the way managers and employees interact. Some are participative and involve employees making decisions that might have been made by a manager or supervisor in more traditional organizations. In other cases, the relationships are more consultative – employees make suggestions, but mangers make the ultimate decisions. In some cases, employees merely act on instructions given by managers. Therefore, empowerment, as a management technique, can be confusing and covers really quite different experiences for employees and managers.

The work of Conger and Kanungo (1989) is helpful because they define empowerment as being both relational and motivational. Their model is useful because it allows initiatives that alter the relationship between the manager and the managed to be considered, and also takes into account those initiatives that leave the relationship structurally unchanged, but which do produce feelings of empowerment.

Table 11.1 suggests that empowerment takes a number of forms which identify different relationships between managers and those they are aiming to empower. **Empowerment through Participation** covers a number of initiatives whereby employees make decisions that would previously have been made by a manager or supervisor. **Empowerment through involvement** includes initiatives that are mostly consultative, when employees are asked for their ideas and suggestions, but managers make the final decision. **Empowerment through commitment** describes arrangements that are attempting to engage employee feelings of empowerment in structures that are traditionally command and control orientated. **Empowerment through Delayering** is largely concerned with the organizational hierarchy by removing levels and making the structure 'flatter'. In these circumstances, junior managers or frontline staff take on certain decision making roles that would usually belong to their more senior colleagues.

Table 11.1	Managerial Meanings of Empowerment	
Managerial Meaning	**Initiatives Used**
Empowerment through participation	Autonomous work groups
	'Whatever it takes' training
	Job enrichment
	Works council
	Employee directors
Empowerment through involvement	Quality circles
	Team briefings
	Suggestion schemes
Empowerment through commitment	Employee share ownership
	Profit sharing and bonus
	Schemes
	Quality of working life programmes:
	– Job rotation
	– Job enlargement (sub-points?)
Empowerment through 'delayering'	Job re-design
	Re-training
	Autonomous work groups
	Job enrichment
	Profit sharing and bonus schemes

Whilst these differences in managerial meanings of empowerment result in different working arrangements and relationships between managers and staff, the key defining feature of empowerment is that people feel empowered. In Conger and Kanungo's terms, they engage with the motivational dimension of empowerment. If empowerment could be differentiated from other employment initiatives, it would engage employees at an emotional level and would be individual and personal. Empowerment is about discretion, autonomy, power and control.

Whatever the intentions of management, the effectiveness of empowerment as an employment strategy is determined by the perceptions, experiences and feelings of the 'empowered'. Fundamentally, these feelings will be rooted in a sense of personal worth and ability to effect outcomes – of having the 'power' to make a difference.

■ Empowered employees are supposed to feel in greater control (Koberg et al., 1999),

■ They have a greater sense of personal power together with the freedom to use that power (Potterfield, 1999),

- They have a sense of personal efficacy and self-determination (Alpander, 1991).

- They have to feel that they have power

- They can make a difference and can exercise choice (Johnson, 1993).

- Unlike disempowered or powerless employees, empowerment provides employees with a sense of

- autonomy,

- authority and

- control (Heslin, 1999)

- together with the abilities, resources and discretion to make decisions. Empowerment, therefore, claims to produce an emotional state in employees from which the additional commitment and effort stem.

As all service organizations increasingly require frontline service personnel to manage their emotions to make them appropriate to any given situation, management use employment practices to create an emotional culture that is consistent with that being presented to customers (Leidner, 1993). Through recruitment, selection, socialization and performance evaluation, organizations develop a social reality in which feelings become a commodity for achieving instrumental goals (Putnam and Munby, 1993: 37). The use of employee empowerment might also be added to this list. Bearing in mind that empowerment takes a variety of forms, it is hoped that, in general, initiatives that involve employees and enable them to participate in decision making, would generate high levels of commitment to the organization on the part of employees. Through empowerment, employees can have an increased sense of 'ownership' of the service encounter resulting in their being able to demonstrate the required emotional responses to customers more easily and with genuine feeling. In terms of the model outlined in Table 11.1, empowerment has the potential to produce emotional harmony. Empowered employees deliver greater customer satisfaction because they are able to respond quickly to customer service needs, but they are also happier in their work and present customers with service interactions that reflect their happiness.

Key learning point 11.4

Empowering frontline staff to provide guests with the emotional service experience they want is a vital aspect of building competitive advantage in a resort

MANAGING AS THOUGH PEOPLE MATTER

This chapter argues that the management of people in hospitality operations has some important differentiating features. Hospitality in timeshare property experiences requires employees to produce performances that meet customer needs on an emotional level. Thus, the management of employees has to be consistent with practice that will contribute to the creation of appropriate emotional dimensions to the customer experience. Table 11.2 lists some of the key concerns of human resource management that, if managed properly, can lead to service excellence in hospitality operations. Ensuring that jobs are designed in a way that encourages positive experiences, recruiting and selecting the right kind of people, ensuring that skills are developed and that performance is monitored and rewarded in a systematic and consistent manner are all important.

Over recent years, many firms in the service sector have undergone processes of re-designing jobs in a way that deskills the work. Job holders can complete job tasks with limited skills, and requiring low levels of training. Recruitment is easier because there is a potentially large pool of labour available. Pay rates are lower and training costs are lower. These trends have been called 'McDonaldization' (Ritzer, 1993, 2003) but they essentially involve techniques first developed in manufacturing. The term 'scientific management' as defined by Taylor (1947) refers to an approach to management that includes re-designing jobs into small component parts with individuals specializing in one small part of the job. As Ritzer's term implies, McDonald's is an obvious example of the application of these techniques, but

Table 11.2	Key Concerns of Human Resource Management in Hospitality Operations	
Personnel Practice	**Personnel Practice**
Job design	Skills and discretion required
Job description	Describing the job to be done
Staff specification	Describing the ideal recruit
Staff specification	Source of potential employees
Recruitment	Attracting suitable applicants
Recruitment	Choosing the right person
Inducting	Settling the person
Training	Developing required skills
Appraisal	Reinforcing and extending performance
Reward and development	Motivating

many other organizations are re-designing their offer to customers, and the jobs need to service them in ways that extend 'efficiency, calculability, predictability and control' (Ritzer, 1993). Although the processes involved appear to be rational, there is an *irrational dimension* to supposedly rational decisions, and high staff turnover and low levels of employee satisfaction experienced by many hospitality and tourism organizations are, in part, caused by job designs which produce low skilled, boring, and monotonous work experiences.

Designing and defining the job

It is important that jobs designed for people allow some degree of autonomy or individual interpretation in them so that employees are less likely to be bored. Several techniques were developed in manufacturing that can be applied to hospitality organizations.

- **Job enrichment** is a technique that partially overlaps with 'participative forms of empowerment'. Jobs are re-designed to build skills and judgements back into the work so that job holders have more autonomy to make decisions that are appropriate to the job.

- **Job enlargement** involves broadening the scope of jobs. So the skill levels and decision making are relatively simple, but the job is enlarged to include more tasks at the same level. The aim is to create more interest, because the job involves a wide range of tasks. Job rotation involves moving people around different jobs. Again the jobs themselves remain largely simple and require limited judgements, but individuals are moved around jobs so as to reduce boredom and monotony.

- Some organizations in hospitality and tourism use **job rotation** to good effect. By creating a **functionally flexible workforce**, they are able move individuals between jobs as demands shift and change. Studies on hotel productivity (Jones, 2002) found that this approach to job design reduced the number employees required to produce the same level of customer sales and service.

Before activating the recruitment process, it is important to systematically define the job and duties involved, and the ideal candidate required. Frequently, recruitment and retention problems in hospitality and tourism operations occur because managers do not take the time to describe the job to be done and the duties involved. The Job Description defines the job; it includes the job title, the position in the hierarchy – job superior and subordinates (where appropriate), the main duties, occasional duties, as well as potential limits on authority. The job description is a rational outline of the job to be done. It can be used in the recruitment process and in the development of individuals.

The **Staff Specification describes** the ideal candidate. Typically this includes consideration of those factors that are essential, and those that are desirable, across areas such as physical make up, education and training, work experience, personality, and personal circumstances. The Staff Specification is helpful because it provides a blueprint of the sort of person who will be able to undertake the duties outlined in the job description. It can help prevent recruitment practices that select the best of the bunch rather than the person who meets the needs of the job to be done. A common problem experienced in hospitality and tourism firms is that recruitment is hurried and not focused on a systematic understanding of the job to be done and the sort of person needed to do it.

Attracting recruits

Before commencing the recruitment process, it is worth considering the labour market. Any one hospitality operation may be recruiting from a number of different labour markets.

- Cleaners and others **undertaking routine unskilled** labour are likely to be recruited from the local area. There is likely to be minimal travel involved. It is important to consider current pay and reward levels being paid by competitors. Employers are sometimes unaware of how the rates being paid measure up against those being offered by firms in not just competitor hospitality firms, but also in the retail, leisure and other sectors. Whilst these employees are potentially plentiful, many other employers are offering jobs of a similar type. A UK study (Lashley et al., 2002) found that hospitality firms were finding it difficult to retain staff because their rates were often 25 per cent below the rates being paid in competitor firms.

- Maintenance, receptionist, and chefs may be recruited from a slightly different labour market, because they are **more skilled**. Fewer staff are needed for these roles than for the routine unskilled labour discussed before. As a result, there may be more obvious competition for these jobs, and the candidates may travel from slightly further a field, or may be recruited with an accommodation package, whereby they live on site.

- **Mangers, sales and marketing** staff may be different again, in that they are fewer in number and may be recruited from a more regional, or even national labour market. Again a clear understanding of competitive terms and conditions is required. A failure to match market rates may result in recruitment difficulties, or problems retaining staff once recruited.

In all cases, recruitment and retention difficulties are increased in times of low unemployment. More competition for people looking for work and more alternatives for existing employees increase the competitive pressures. Some firms deliberately position themselves as being employer of first choice, by paying better wages and having better employment terms and career prospects (Lashley et al., 2002). This enables them to have the pick of staff and retain existing employees more easily.

Before exploring external sources of recruits, it is worth noting that, for some posts, internal sources may be appropriate. Moving individuals from casual to full-time employment, or promoting from within can be both a quick way of filling vacancies and can have a motivating effect on the workforce because it demonstrates the potential for career development. Asking existing staff if they know someone who might be interested in applying for the post is another potential internal source of recruits. This has the advantage of building team links and group dynamics as the recruits and existing staff are known to each other. Whilst the benefits of internal recruitment are important, there can be major disadvantages. The point is to recruit the person who best matches the job requirement, and perhaps there is no one suitable in the organization. In other cases, recruiters are looking for new people who will bring in fresh ideas and skills from other employers.

Once the decision to recruit externally has been taken, the source and method of advertising is decided. Typically, the more specialized the post to be filled, the more likely that post will be advertised using wide circulation media and display advertisements. When recruiting management personnel, or sales and marketing staff, it is likely that job advertisements will be placed in regional, national or trade journals. Advertisements for cleaners, bar and restaurant staff may well be placed in the local paper using classified advertisements (Mullins, 2002).

Good job advertisements are designed to attract sufficient suitable applications for the recruitment process to make a successful appointment. The advertisement should, therefore, target specific candidates, create an interest in the candidates for the post, stimulate a desire to follow up, and inform the candidates how to apply and if there is a deadline for applications.

Once applications have been received, the applicants need to be sifted and matched against the Staff Specification so as to decide on the short-list of candidates to be interviewed. If the advertising process has been successful all applicants should be suitable on paper, though there may be differences in the extent that they match desirable and essential qualities required from the Staff Specification. Recruiters use many techniques to assist in the short-listing process, but the key requirement is to be objective and fair. Usually a system using a scoring process and involving more than one person making the selection overcomes some of the potential bias. Ethical recruitment processes avoid pre-judgements and filtering people on superficial grounds, such as ethnicity, gender or on the grounds of disability. Ultimately, the process has to be open to ethical scrutiny.

The selection process

At its most basic, the selection of candidates for employment involves some form of interviewing process. Interviews are by far the most widely used selection technique. Interviewers feel comfortable with the process, though research suggests that this confidence is often misplaced. There is a tendency for interviewers to adopt a number of techniques which can result in over-emphasizing the strengths of some candidates and the weaknesses of others. Some organizations try to overcome these problems by the use of more than one interviewer and one interview. In other cases, selection decisions are informed by aptitude and attitude tests, personality profiles and/or role plays. The use of Emotional Intelligence Quotients is one example of a test being used by some firms in the sector.

- Pret a Manager, a UK based sandwich chain, recruit new staff only after the individual has worked with the team for a shift and the team elect to recommend appointment.

- In TGI Fridays, new staff are subject to as many as four interviews and role play situations.

Where interviews are used as part of the selection process, it is important to approach interviews in a planned and coordinated fashion. Before the interviews the interviewing team need to decide on the structure and timing of the interview that they are familiar with, and have allocated sufficient time for the interviewing to take place. During the interview, it is important that candidates are given a chance to show their strengths and questions are asked in a way that encourages a discussion. The management of the interview should allow sufficient time for each candidate and recognize that the interview is a two-way process whereby the candidate is also selecting the firm. After the interview, interviewers need to make the selection in a rational manner. Again, a scoring system can be useful, because it enables a decision to be made on the basis of viewing the candidate in the context of the job requirements, as defined in the job specification.

References supporting the candidate's application can be taken up before or after the interviewing process. Clearly, references supplied prior to the interviews can help support the selection process. Those taken after interviews are being used to verify and confirm the impressions gained at the interview. In both cases, references are not always strictly accurate. In some cases, referees are loathed to be overly critical of an applicant. In other cases, referees may be giving an unrealistically favourable picture of the applicant because of personal ties or because an existing employer wants to be rid of an unsuitable employee.

> **Key learning point 11.5**
> Careful recruitment and selection of employees is an essential step in ensuring that timeshare operations retain the services of a productive and loyal workforce capable of meeting the physical and emotional needs of guests.

Induction and employment

Once the successful candidate has been selected, it is important to plan an induction programme for the new recruit. Induction programmes should formally introduce the recruit to the organization, work colleagues and role. A well-planned induction programme recognizes that the new recruit has anxieties and needs, and that the programme is as concerned with meeting these needs as it is with making the recruit an efficient employee as quickly as possible. The induction programme may extend over several days and weeks, covering a range of issues that will help the recruit in understanding the organization and their role within it.

- Lashley and Best (2001) found that many hospitality firms claimed to have an induction programme, but this was often limited to legislative requirements. Some firms had a **structured programme** that identified a range of skills and competences to be developed. In other cases, the programmes were **informal and restricted** to showing new recruits the basic job tasks. In none of the surveyed firms did the induction programme address the emotional needs of the recruit.

Induction training is part of the induction process and is essentially concerned with ensuring that employees learn the skills required to be effective in the job. Formal training, which has clear objectives and structures, tends to enable recruits to be effective more quickly and achieve higher levels of long term output (Eaglen et al., 2000).

Research on the benefits and costs of training and development (Eaglen et al., 1999) shows that employee training produces an array of **business benefits** including increased employee productivity.

- Although productivity is a complex concept in hospitality services, formally trained frontline service staff tend to *serve more customers* and have *higher average transaction values* than employees who learn in informal ways.

- In addition, they register higher levels of personal job satisfaction,

- produce better service quality and

- have more satisfied customers.

- They are also more confident, more flexible and more likely to accept change.

This range of benefits covers both tangible and intangible benefits and a problem faced by many hospitality and tourism firms is that performance management systems are frequently limited to financial performance. Often, they are incapable of capturing the benefits flowing from training and development and as a consequence tend to see training as a luxury.

- In reality, **not providing training is costly**, and leads to *lower productivity, higher staff turnover* and *lower customer satisfaction* (Eaglen and Lashley, 2001).

Ongoing staff performance appraisal helps to produce a climate of continuous professional development. The development of individuals ensures that individuals are performing effectively, but control of individuals should not be the main motive for appraisal systems.

Best practice suggests that appraisal is primarily concerned with development and gaining insights into the appraisee's experiences and ambitions.

- In some cases, a 360 degree process involves the staff member appraising the manager as well as the manager appraising the employee.

- Appraisal systems vary in their scope and frequency; typically, they occur on an annual basis, though in some instances the appraisal takes place more regularly – every six months or so.

- Appraisals assist communication processes between staff and managers, and ensures that employee aspirations are understood by managers.

This helps ensure that employee frustrations are minimized and, most importantly, that managers understand sources of satisfaction and rewards that are most appealing to staff.

Rewards from work can be identified under two headings. *Extrinsic rewards* originate outside of the individual. They are best understood as material rewards in the form of

- bonus schemes,

- tips,

- commission,

- performance related pay,

- share option schemes and so on.

Research shows that managers have a general tendency to consider these incentives more important to employees than they are in reality to employees (Lashley, 2000). That is not to say that people won't want to improve their income. However, people are not usually driven to maximize material rewards at all costs. Most people strike an effort–reward bargain, whereby they will increase work effort to increase income to a point. In addition, financial incentives can distort the priorities pursued by individuals, because individuals may prioritize those activities which maximize income at the expense of other outcomes.

- For example, sales personnel in some timeshare firms have been criticized for being overly concerned to make a sale with the use of high pressure sales techniques. Commission-linked sales targets may result in sales made, but some poor public relations impacts and ultimately dissatisfied customers.

Intrinsic rewards are those rewards from work which do not materially benefit the individual, but make the post holder better off.

- The nature of the work itself,

- feeling in control,

- feeling effective and having the skills needed for the job

are all influences that help a person feel good about their work.

Rodwell et al. (1998) suggest that several surveys show that employee satisfaction levels are positively linked to personal autonomy and having some degree of choice over how tasks are completed. Effective communications is also a key ingredient in enabling employees to clearly understand what is expected of them and where the organization is going. The role of immediate supervisors is also positively linked to employee satisfaction levels (Argenti, 1998). The supervisor's management style and praising of subordinates has a key impact on generating these intrinsic rewards from work. Concerns to re-design jobs in the ways outlined earlier are all examples of approaches to job design which are enhancing intrinsic rewards from work:

■ empowerment,

■ job enrichment,

■ job enlargement,

■ job rotation and

■ emotional leadership

are all linked in different ways to helping employees feel better about work.

> **Key learning point 11.6**
> Systematic employment practices, training and good rewards which recognize intrinsic and extrinsic factors give existing employees reasons to stay and may attract others from competitor organizations. Being employer of first choice underpins a strategy of building competitive advantage to the excellence of service quality in the resort.

SUMMARY

This chapter has argued that human resource management practices have a crucial contribution to make to timeshare service operations, because of the emotional dimensions present in the decision by customers to use commercial hospitality services. Fundamentally, the links between the emotions of hospitality and the performance given by frontline staff require careful consideration and management. The chapter suggests that these considerations need to go beyond the current practice of demanding an emotional element to employees' performance as exemplified by the 'Have a nice day' culture. Important though this is, these emotional demands can lead to emotional disharmony, emotional labour and added job stress which feeds into more staff turnover and poor service levels.

Empowerment of frontline staff has the potential to provide a set of management techniques that support staff and enable them to deliver the emotional performance required of hospitality service. Empowerment, however, is not just a quick fix. It means a number of different things and managers need to understand the different meanings of empowerment and choose the most appropriate form to suit the performance needed. Typically, participative forms of empowerment are most suited to the delivery of high quality services whereby visitors feel the full warmth of the traditional Irish welcome.

Given the key significance of employee and management performance to customer satisfaction levels, and ultimately to the ability of organizations to build competitive advantage through quality customer experiences, the management of people has a central significance. The design of jobs in the first instance, and the recruitment of the most suitable employees, their development and reward are issues to be carefully planned and executed. People are more than a production cost to be minimized so as to extract extra profit. People are the key assets of the hospitality industry and need to be recognized as such through the use of techniques that are built into organizational performance review.

CHAPTER 12

Condominium Hotels

After working through this chapter, you should be able to

- identify why condominium hotels are attractive to consumers and developers

- understand the increase in interest in condominium ownership by foreign investors

- understand the growth and the brands associated with the growth in condominium hotel development

- understand how condominium hotels are financed by the consumer

INTRODUCTION

Condominium hotels have been defined as 'typically high-rise buildings developed and operated as luxury hotels, usually in major cities, in the US and around the world. These hotels have condominium units which allow someone to own a full-service vacation home that they can use whenever they like. When they aren't using this home, the owner can leverage the marketing and management of the hotel chain to rent and manage the condo unit as it would any other hotel room' (Chin, 2007).

Condominium hotels that are being developed are not your typical second home. The furnishings are pricing and the locations are in urban as well as resort areas. The hotels are typically high-rise, luxury properties with prices ranging from $250 000 to over $1 million. The condo hotel owner is attracted to a product that gives them a vacation home whenever they want to use it

CONTENTS

with more amenities than you would find at a traditional condominium. Because they are operated as hotels, one would find the availability of a valet, concierge, and daily maid service.

CONDOMINIUM HOTELS

The branded condominium hotel unit owners that are affiliated with major hotel companies can take advantage of the rental program when the unit is not in use by the owner (this is the same with non-branded condominium hotels as well). The major advantage of being part of the brand is once in the rental pool, although the developer does not guarantee the rental of the unit, the owner can capitalize on the hotel's name recognition, advertising, national affiliations, centralized reservation system, and management expertise which should bring more exposure to the units that are in the rental pool and therefore attract a larger audience much more so than a traditional vacation home.

Typically condo hotel company rental agreements state that the hotel pays for most of the operating expenses (housekeeping, administrative, and marketing) and the condo hotel owner is responsible for real estate taxes, insurance, and capital improvements.

Top 10 reasons to buy a condo hotel unit are as follows:

1. *Vacation 'free' anytime:* When you own a condo hotel unit, you can use your vacation home anytime.

2. *Enjoy luxury accommodations:* Most condo hotels are high-end properties with a great deal of amenities. They are operated by some of the most respected names in the hospitality industry such as Hilton, Starwood, and Sonesta.

3. *Avoid maintenance headaches:* Unlike when you own a second home or condo, when you own a condo hotel unit, the management company takes care of day to day maintenance. You get a great vacation home without dealing with maintenance headaches.

4. *Secure your place in the sun:* Places with prime beach real estates such as locations in South Florida have been completely built up. Buying a condo hotel unit secures a prime place for recreation for now and for the future.

5. *Generate rental income:* When you are not using your condo hotel unit you may place it in the hotel's rental program. The hotel management company then places it in the pool to be rented. After expenses, the profit is split amongst the owners that have units in the rental pool.

6. *Get in on the bottom of the condo hotel craze:* Although the success of condo hotels is not known yet, many people are getting on board in the hope that they are buying the next best thing in real estate.

7. *Gain appreciation potential:* The babyboomers that drove up traditional real estate prices in the housing market are now beginning to purchase in the condo hotel market. International buyers (the British, Mexicans, Latin Americans, and Canadians) are also shopping in the US for second homes. Based on real estate history, when a rapidly growing number of people with desire and wealth focus their buying power traditionally, the cost of real estate goes up.

8. *Secure easy mortgage financing:* Currently lenders like the condo hotel concept, so it is easier to secure financing.

9. *Save on taxes:* There is a possibility to save money on taxes by owning a second home. Federal tax deductions and tax sheltered income are possible in some instances. Also, in some cases, various property taxes, income taxes, and other fees have been reduced or eliminated by state or local governments.

10. *Diversify your investments:* The stock market can be unpredictable and second home prices have been forecasted to appreciate in many locations. Real estate adds diversity to a person's investment portfolio.

September 11, 2001 terrorist attacks exacerbated the decline of lender support in the hospitality industry and led many developers to sell off some of their inventory as condominiums. Lenders began to find the condo hotel concept favourable because of the addition of pre-sale capital from potential owners that help to pay down construction loans. The lenders that once would only loan 60 per cent of the value of the hotel (60 per cent loan to value) would now loan 75 per cent (75 per cent loan to value) if the hotel had a condominium component. The rate of return over the standard hotel project is typically 15 per cent and with a condominium component, the rate of return can be doubled. Today, it is increasingly being found that many lenders will not look at a luxury hotel project if there is no condominium component involved.

The benefits of the condo hotel concept to the hotel owners and operators are as follows:

1. Access to financing is easier than as a hotel.

2. Marketing costs are lower because each unit they are selling to one owner, not 51 or 52.

3. Condo hotel units provide additional room inventory.

Some of the cons of owning a condo hotel versus a traditional condominium are that most communities restrict the amount of time an owner can stay in their unit during a stay. Usually after 3–4 weeks, the owner must vacate. The reasoning behind this is that normally the condo hotel is in a prime tourism area and they want to make certain that the hotel is being used by tourists as well and not being used as a permanent home.

There are other restrictions including not being able to have personal designer touches and complying with the hotel guidelines with regards to installing any kind of furniture. There is less flexibility because of the need to tell the hotel within a certain time period when they will be using the unit. Also if the owner places their unit into a rental pool, they lose control over who rents their condominium. In a resort location there may be people renting that want to have too much of a good time and cause a great deal of wear and tear on the condominium.

Some prospective condo hotel owners have reservations about buying. The condo hotel is a small space for the amount of money that they are spending, most units average 600–700 square feet (the trade off is the amenities that you would not typically find at a traditional condominium development and a full time staff that is in place to rent the hotel room for the owner). Another concern is that even though they can put their unit in a rental pool, the size and type (view, no-view, etc.) can affect the popularity of their unit and in turn affect their rental income.

Some other limitations to owning a condo hotel include the following:

- *Reservation requirements:* to ensure availability of the unit, owners need to let the hotel know in advance, sometimes as much as 60 days before their stay.

- *Unit conformity:* units come fully-furnished according to the hotel's decor and standards and changes are not allowed. Sometimes, owners are held responsible for periodic furniture replacement as well.

- *The inconvenience of packing for your own vacation home:* personal items such as clothes, personal effects, photos, cannot be left in the unit unless there is an owner's closet.

Other limitations apply regardless of your participation in the rental program:

- *Living restrictions:* some hotels and some local governments put limits on the amount of time owners can stay in their unit in a given year (to ensure hotel capacity and hotel visitor tax income).

- *Lack of transparency:* under SEC regulations, if the seller stresses the investment potential, it comes under SEC jurisdiction, rules and restrictions, and is taxed as an investment. Therefore, condo developers uniformly do not provide important data such as room rates and occupancy levels which would help estimate potential rental income. This can make the purchase decision more difficult (Helium Report, 2007).

Key learning point 12.1

Condominium hotel development is a fast growing trend with many selling points for the perspective vacation home owner. If the owner understands the pros and cons of condominium hotel ownership and their vacation needs are met through ownership a win–win relationship can occur between condominium hotel owner and hotel developer.

CASE STUDY

Alan and Celeste are avid vacationers; they spend at least one month out of the year travelling. Recently, they have heard about condominium hotels and are interested in learning more about them. Although, their travels take them around the world, they have found that they love spending time in South Florida and are looking to invest in a vacation home in the area.

They set up an appointment with a local realtor who showed them many different vacation homes some of which included units in condominium hotels. Alan and Celeste were intrigued with the services offered by the condominium hotel (on-site restaurant with room service and a full-service gym) but wanted to know more about

the condominium hotel industry before making such a big decision that could prove costly if they did not do their homework.

Alan and Celeste were looking for a vacation home to call their own and are interested in a vacation home with all of the services of a luxury hotel. Their schedules are flexible so they know well in advance when they would want to use their home and they never plan on staying in the condominium more than two weeks at a time. However, Celeste had loves to decorate and is wary of living somewhere without having the ability to design their home and Alan wants to make certain they are investing in a vacation home that will appreciate in value.

Reflective practice

1. Read the case study and determine why Alan and Celeste would be interested in condo hotel ownership and why not.

2. What other questions would you need to ask to determine whether they would be well suited for condo hotel ownership?

3. If you were going to market to Alan and Celeste, what are some key areas that you would focus on to show them why condo hotel ownership would work for them.

GROWTH IN FOREIGN INTEREST AND BRANDS

In South Florida although talk of a downturn in the traditional condominium market is evident, the gap in the supply of luxury condo hotels is still falling short of demand. There is potential for overbuilding in the luxury condo market, but the lack of developable waterfront property has limited the opportunity to overdevelop at this point. There are many choices which encourage potential condo hotel unit owners to look in the area.

Based on the fact that the stock market is depressed, CD, money-market funds, and income-producing securities are showing historically low rates and many people are looking to the real estate market for investing. Florida real estate prices have been escalating. The Florida real estate market made it through post September 11th better than expected because of mortgage rates, lack of suitable alternative investment opportunities, and the influx of capital and people from Latin America and the Caribbean.

The number of German property investors is growing for South Florida condo hotel projects. The tax savings and the strengthening of the Euro are causing the Germans to renew their interest in US real estate markets. Germans like the alternative of owning a piece of real estate that generates rental income where management of the facility is taken care of. In 2002, there was a change in the German tax law that made owning foreign real estate much more attractive. In Germany, there are not enough opportunities for investment proportional to the amount of savings that are generated. The German potential real estate investor sees US real estate as a well priced investment that will offer secure cash flow with the potential for appreciation.

A driver of the condo hotel trends is the fact that lenders are wary about funding development of four and five star hotels. High construction cost has resulted in an average four or five star hotel costing $400 000 per hotel room to build. Regardless of the development sponsorship many lenders have decided the risk is too great. Condo hotels are more popular for potential owners from outside the US because of their familiarity with the product. Condo hotels have been an option in Europe and Latin America for years.

South Florida is seen as an ideal place because of the influx of Latin business people that would rather spend the money on owning rather than renting. There has been an increase in properties that not only contain hotel rooms they include office space as well to make the property even more attractive to this market. They are marketing the properties as one stop shopping. A place to house your business as well as lodging for employees or clients of the business encourages efficiency by having everything in one place.

The appeal of US property to foreign investors

The attractiveness of condo hotels by foreign investors is clear. They have become a greatly sought after market based on their desire for real estate in the US. There are many advantages to own U.S. real estate from the foreign investors' vantage point. Some of the advantages include the following (Helium Report, 2007):

1. Diversifying their investments in something that is not tied to the health of their own domestic economy.

2. The US has a wide selection of real estate that is available for investment with a high turnover rate that makes exiting easier. The US is less restrictive with property purchased by foreigners than other countries.

3. Real estate is less exposed to the results of inflation than other investments and often rises more than the rate of inflation.

4. Changes in technology have created more opportunities for foreign investors. With the help of technology monitoring potential investments and purchasing has gotten to be much quicker and easier.

Brands and condominium hotels

The **Mandarin Oriental** located above the Time Warner Center in New York City is selling condos up to $3000 a square foot which results in a $12 million dollar condominium with three bedrooms, a maid's room, and a library. The Ritz Carlton, New York, located at 50 Central Park South, has condos from $12 million to $28 million. Not all luxury condo hotels have price tags in the millions. Ritz Carlton in Washington, DC, has condos starting at $600 000. Four Seasons has a San Francisco property that starts at $700 000.

The **Hilton chain's** luxury brand has committed to greatly expanding its portfolio of destinations and condo hotels represent a significant part of the financing strategy of this expansion (Helium Report, 2007).

Notable projects include the following:

■ *Conrad Majestic [Las Vegas, NV]* has 696 condo hotel suites ranging in size from 630 to 1200 square feet and initially priced from approximately $650k to $1.5m.

■ *Conrad Dubai [Dubai, UAE]* has 130 units on Sheikh Zayed Road in the heart of Dubai's commercial, business and entertainment district.

- *Conrad Koh Samui [Koh Samui, Thailand]* has 39 residential villas each starting at 2000 square feet in size spread out on 25 acres with panoramic views of the Gulf of Thailand.

The hotel casino operator made news for selling out all 576 units of its first phase Signature project at blazing speeds in 2004, and now has embarked on another Las Vegas landmark project called CityCenter (Helium Report, 2007).

Notable projects include the following:

- *Vdara [Las Vegas, NV]* has 1543 units at $7 billion MGM CityCenter project on the Las Vegas Strip. Sizes ranging from studios at 500 square feet to multi-level penthouse suites at 1850 square feet, pricing between $500 000 and $3 million.

- *Signature at MGM Grand [Las Vegas, NV]* has three towers of condo units ranging in size from studios to two bedrooms adjoining the casino hotel.

Starwood features its W Hotel brand on condo hotel projects with the W's familiar chic design aesthetic and amenities such as Bliss Spa (Helium Report, 2007).

Notable projects include the following:

- *The W South Beach [Miami, FL]* has 511 studio, one- and two-bedroom units ranging in size from 564 to 1287 square feet with prices starting at $740 000.

- *The W Fort Lauderdale [Fort Lauderdale, FL]* has 171 units on Ft. Lauderdale Beach. One-bedroom units priced from $975 000 and two-bedroom units from $1 290 900.

With a brand associated with international luxury, **Trump** is building out a roster of condo hotel locations throughout the US and beyond (Helium Report, 2007).

Notable projects include the following:

- *Trump SoHo [New York, NY]* has 407 condo hotel units ranging in size from 430 square feet to 800 square feet. Several penthouse units will also be included.

- *Trump Ocean Club [Panama City, Panama]* has approximately 300 units in a waterfront mixed use development including casino and yacht club. Prices starting at less than $400k.

- *Trump Hotel Waikiki [Honolulu, HI]* has 460 condo hotel units ranging in size from 562 square feet studios to 2110 square feet three-bedroom units. Prices from under $500k to nearly $3 million.

- *Trump Ocean Resort Baja Mexico* has studio, one-, two-, and three-bedroom condo hotel units, ranging in size from 700 to 4500 square feet about 30 minutes from San Diego, CA.

- *The Palm Trump International Hotel & Tower Dubai [Dubai, UAE]* has at the trunk of the palm-shaped Jumeirah island, one of the world's largest man-made islands. Approximately 500 units ranging from one-, two-, three-bedroom suites and penthouses.

Key learning point 12.2

The condominium hotel concept is international in nature and is gaining ground as foreign investors are looking to diversify their portfolio.

CASE STUDY

Alan and Celeste were impressed to see that so many international brand hotel companies are developing condominium hotels. They have been less than impressed with their return on investments in the stock market and are curious to determine whether owning a condominium hotel would be a good investment. Ironically, they found out that although purchasing a piece of real estate is generally considered an investment, condominium hotels cannot be sold as investment properties because of regulations with the Security Exchange Commission.

This made Alan and Celeste wonder as to what are the benefits of buying a traditional vacation home where there have been proven track records in appreciation in the area that they are looking at and purchasing a unit in a condominium hotel which is an unknown entity. They kept going back and forth trying to determine whether they would be in on the ground floor of an exciting concept or should they go with a more traditional choice?

Reflective practice

1. What is the impact of foreign investments on condominium hotels? How do you think it would benefit a community?

2. What kind of person would be a better candidate to purchase a unit in a condominium hotel? Do you visualize a specific type of market the developer should focus on?

3. What questions do you think Alan and Celeste should be asking to determine what would be the best vacation home concept for their family?

FINANCING CONDOMINIUM HOTELS

Buying a condo hotel unit is similar to buying a traditional condominium, but there are a few extra considerations to understand. These will be discussed in the following section. To qualify for a condo hotel loan, most lenders look at the loan as similar to financing an investment property and qualify you based on your income. However, unlike traditional investment properties, the lenders do not count potential rental income from the condo hotel unit towards qualifying for a loan.

Lenders may also need to pre-approve the condominium hotel project as a whole before making the loan. However, as condo hotel loans have become more common, there have been less hoops to jump through. Projects that have not been pre-approved, may have a stipulation that 75 per cent of the condo hotel units must be under contract before they make a loan. Some lenders have minimum unit size requirements of 600 square feet. Based on the fact, the larger the unit the more likely it will rent and make more money on the resale market. Lenders may waive the size requirement if the project has been pre-approved or if it contains at least the basic kitchen facilities.

There are minimum down payments usually 20 per cent of the purchase price and this percentage increases as the price of the condo hotel unit goes up. An example would be 80 per cent loan to value (LTV) up to a $350 000 loan amount and $437 500 maximum purchase price; 75 per cent LTV up to a $650 000 loan amount and $867 000 maximum purchase price; and 45 per cent LTV up to $1 million loan amount and a $2.22 million maximum purchase price. Also, in general any form of secondary financing is not allowed in purchasing a condo hotel unit.

To be pre-approved for a condo hotel loan, you must provide documentation of your income and the bank will check your credit. The average credit score that is acceptable is in the 680 range, but there are always exceptions. Finally, a condo hotel project must be a fee simple project or a leasehold project to be considered for a loan. The definitions are as follows:

Fee simple: Absolute ownership in real property; owner is entitled to the entire property with unconditional power of disposition during the owner's life.

Leasehold: Estate or interest in real property held by the virtue of a lease. Leasehold refers to land which is leased to the individual(s) who owns the structure.

Condo hotel basic financial analysis

Analysing the economics of a condo hotel unit is extremely difficult because of the challenge of getting accurate information about the potential income stream. Developers uniformly do not provide important data or estimates for room rates or occupancy levels for fear of coming under SEC regulations on investments, as opposed to real estate regulations (Table 12.1).

However, using some basic assumptions, it is possible to get a rough idea for the economics of a condo hotel:

Step 1: estimating income – The key assumptions in the estimation of income are as follows:

- *Rental rate:* Within a hotel, the rate may also vary due to unit size, floor, location in building (views).

- *Occupancy:* Reservations are rotated among available units; however, guest requests such as room size or view take priority.

- *Personal usage:* This is sometimes limited by hotel policy or local laws.

Step 2: Estimating costs – The key assumptions in the estimation of costs are as follows:

- *Franchise fees:* Typically 10–12 per cent of gross rental income.

- *Management fees:* Varies depending on developer and even project.

- *Monthly maintenance fees:* Based on the size of the unit.

- *Capital expenditures:* The management company will often hold 5 per cent of revenue as a reserve used to replace or upgrade unit furnishings.

Table 12.1   Market Ranges in the Condo Hotel Industry

Market Ranges

Property prices	Typically anywhere from $500 000 to $5 million
Occupancy (%)	50–90
Franchise fee (% of gross rent)	10–12
Management fee split (% of gross rent)	40–55
Monthly maintenance (per sq ft; $)	1.00–1.50
Down payment required (%)	20–30

Source: Helium Report 2007

Helium report example

The example is a one-bedroom suite that is a representation of the many condo hotel projects available. The assumptions are conservative, but they do show the impact of the franchise and management fees (Table 12.2).

Using the unit for 15 days of the year, an occupancy rate of 65 per cent for the times it is otherwise available, and market average fee structures produces a negative return on assets of slightly more than 3 per cent. In other words, the unit's rental income does not fully cover the ownership costs and the owner would need to continue to invest in the property. However, given appreciation of the condo unit which is in-line with recent trends in desirable markets (15 per cent year over year), results in a still significant financial benefit from ownership of over 11 per cent in annual returns (Helium Report, 2007; Table 12.3).

Understanding the numbers

Therefore, the reason why people would be interested in condo hotel ownership is the possibility of making money through the appreciation of the

Table 12.2	Assumptions for Condo Hotel Investment Example
Helium Report Assumptions	
Condo details	
Size (sq ft)	1000
Monthly maintenance (per sq ft; $)	1.25
Purchase details	
Purchase price ($)	1 000 000
Down payment (%)	30
Mortgage rate (30 yr; %)	7.00
Other ownership expenses	
Real estate property taxes (% of purchase price)	2
Insurance	
Hotel details	
Average daily rate ($)	650
Occupancy (%)	65
Franchise fee (% of gross rent)	10
Management fee split (% of gross rent)	45
Capital expenditures (often held as reserve; %)	5
Days of personal use	15
Days available to rent per year	350

Source: Helium Report, 2007

Table 12.3	Example of Condo Hotel Investment Spreadsheet		
	Daily	**Monthly**	**Annual**
Income			
Rental rate ($)	650	19 771	237 250
Gross rental revenue ($)	396	12 039	144 463
Expenses			
Franchise fee ($)	39.58	1203.85	14 446.25
Management fees ($)	178.10	5417.34	65 008.13
Monthly maintenance fees ($)	41.10	1250.00	15,000.00
Capital expenditures/improvements ($)	19.79	601.93	7223.13
Mortgage payment ($)	153.11	4657.12	55 885.41
Real estate property taxes ($)	54.79	1666.67	20 000.00
Total expenses ($)	486.47	14 796.91	177 562.91
Net income ($)	90.69	2758.37	33 100.41
Return on assets	−3.31%		
Appreciation	15.00%		
Total rate of return	11.69%		

Source: Helium Report, 2007

property. They expect that the rental income should cover most of the expenses. The high cost of franchise and management fees do cut into the profit and leave two reasons to buy. The experience of owning a vacation home in a luxury hotel and the potential for appreciation without property management hassles.

Cost analysis

The cost of a condo hotel unit is driven by four fees which may vary from development to development and from unit to unit:

1. **Franchise fees**: typically 10–12 per cent of gross rental income.

2. **Management fees**: varies depending on developer and project.

3. **Monthly maintenance fees**: based on the size of the unit.

4. **Capital expenditures**: often 5 per cent of revenue held by management to replace or upgrade unit furnishings (Helium Report, 2007).

Condo hotels face the same ownership risks as any other deeded property. Here are some additional risks that owners bear:

- Dependence on hotel management company's ability to effectively and efficiently manage property while maximizing revenues.

- Long term agreement with hotel management company.

- Frequency of new renters (hotel guests) can create additional wear and tear on unit as well as increase risk of more substantial damage.

- Reservation requirements to ensure availability of the unit; owners need to let the hotel know in advance, sometimes as many as 60 days before their stay.

- Living restrictions: some hotels and some local governments put limits on the amount of time owners can stay in their unit in a given year (to ensure hotel capacity and hotel visitor tax income).

- Lack of transparency: under SEC regulations, if the seller stresses the investment potential, it comes under SEC jurisdiction, rules and restrictions, and is taxed as an investment. Therefore, condo developers uniformly do not provide important data such as room rates and occupancy levels which would help estimate potential rental income. This can make the purchase decision more difficult (Helium Report, 2007).

Questions to ask

Potential owners need to make certain to ask the following questions to determine whether condo hotel ownership is right for them (Helium Report, 2007):

1. Is this purchase primarily for investment or for personal enjoyment?

2. For my investment strategy, do I prioritize rental yield or appreciation?

3. How predictable is my vacation schedule?

4. How important is it for me to design and decorate my home the way I want to?

Key leaning point 12.3

Condominium hotel financing is made more complex because of lack of rental history. The consumer that chooses to purchase a condo hotel unit needs to prioritize what they want to get out of the purchase. The primary goal needs to be that they are purchasing for their own personal enjoyment. The supplemental income made by the rental income should not be depended on to cover all costs.

CASE STUDY

Alan and Celeste have decided that they like the idea of owning a vacation home with all of the amenities of a luxury hotel. They have enough money to cover their mortgage and fees without depending on the rental income to make those payments. They both believe that it will be a wise choice for them; because of their busy schedules, they do not want to worry about day to day issues that may arise and know that they can plan well in advance when they want to use the condo hotel unit. They may even choose to share it with their friends and family as a potential gift on occasion.

Reflective practice

1. Why do you think Alan and Celeste are ideal condominium hotel owners?

2. Based on the information found in the section related to how condominium hotels are financed, what should they double check before they make their final decision when choosing a condominium hotel developer?

3. Based on the information found in the appendix, what questions would you suggest they ask the developer considering what you know of Alan and Celeste and the reason why they are purchasing this unit.

SUMMARY

Condominium hotels have become an appealing option to consumers who wish to have the convenience of hotel services while experiencing ownership at their favourite getaway. This segment has also offered hotel companies a means to expand more rapidly by supplying funds via pre-construction selling. This concept can be a win–win venture for both parties in the right location and when buyers' expectations are met by the developer. Education of the consumer is a necessity to ensure that the consumer is fully capitalized to take part in such a venture and is buying it for the right reasons.

APPENDIX

What to ask – Condo hotel development details

1. Who is the developer? What other condo hotel developments has the developer built?

2. Who is the management company? What other condo hotel developments does this company manage?

3. What is the term of the hotel management contract?

4. What is the state of the local hotel industry (capacity, occupancy, new developments)?

5. What are the planned uses for this development (condo hotel, hotel, residential, retail, commercial)?

6. How many condo units will be included in this development?

7. What is the range in floor plans and sizes of the condo units in this development?

8. Are photos or other examples available of the planned interior decorations?

9. What is the current or planned rating (number of stars) for the hotel?

10. Has the price of the hotel condo units changed during the pre-construction sale period? If so, how often and by how much?

11. What is the payment schedule for pre-construction units? When are deposits due?

12. When are deposits non-refundable?

13. Does this development carry the National Association of Condo Hotel Owners (NACHO) Seal of Approval?

What to ask – condo unit & rental program details

1. What are the positive/negative factors for your unit which may affect occupancy and/or rental rate (view, floor, size, location)?

2. What are the monthly maintenance costs associated with my unit?

3. What is the allowable annual increase in maintenance costs?

4. Will there be any on-site storage available to owners?

5. Are there requirements for minimum amounts of insurance?

6. Are there living restrictions that limit the amount of time per year I can stay in my unit? Are these municipal regulations or hotel management dictated?

7. If I stay beyond my allotted time, does the hotel offer a discounted hotel rate to owners?

8. How much notice do I need to provide to guarantee availability of my unit?

9. Are there any blackout dates during which owners may not stay in their units?

10. What is the procedure and costs associated with opting into or out of the rental program?

11. Are there fees such as departure fees, maid service fees that accrue when I stay in my unit?

12. Which amenities will I have access to during my owner stays? Are there any additional fees for usage?

13. Does the hotel close, limit amenities or otherwise change policies during any seasonal off-season or peak season?

14. What are the franchise fees associated with participation in the rental program?

15. What is the split of rental income between the management and the owner?

16. Is there a reserve from my rental income to cover the costs of capital improvements such as replacing or upgrading furnishings?

17. Are capital expenditures such as upgrading and replacing furnishings shared by management and owner?

18. What hotel operating fees such as marketing costs, travel agent commissions, credit card commissions are shared by the management and owner?

19. How often is rent distributed to owners?

20. How are room reservations rotated in the rental program?

CHAPTER 13

Vacation Ownership Expansion

After working through this chapter, you should be able to

- understand the fractional ownership segment (use rights, locations, and amenities offered).

- understand the destination club segment (use rights, locations, and amenities offered).

- identify the difference between fractional and destination clubs.

- understand the residential cruise line segment (ship profiles, amenities offered, and usage plans.

INTRODUCTION

The success of the timeshare industry has resulted in the expansion of the timeshare concept in a myriad of areas. This chapter will focus on the expansion of timeshare concepts in lodging (Fractionals, Destination Clubs) and cruises. The timeshare concept has expanded to every travel concept that can be offered because of public demand and the money that is made by the suppliers. The travelling public is looking for a carefree way to travel experiencing the best the world has to offer without the headaches involved with maintaining the experience. This chapter will share the alternatives that are present for the travelling public at this point in time. The list continues to evolve to meet the needs of a market that is seeking the best through vacation ownership.

FRACTIONALS

The Fractional concept although it has been around unofficially in some form since the timeshare concept took hold in the late 1960s became a concept that gained popularity in the United States in 1994. The concept was the formalized structure of 12 friends that went in together to share a vacation home, each owner receiving one month of vacation time in the home. Fractional ownership's formalized structure categorizes ownership at a luxury resort in a villa or condominium from 4 to 12 weeks of ownership. Fractional ownership classifies ownership into fourths, eighths, or 13ths. Each owner receives an equal amount of days during the year to use the unit. Fractional ownership has evolved into Private Residence clubs that include five star accommodations and amenities (Aventuras Club, 2008). Research indicates that people that own second homes only spend 3–4 weeks a year in them anyway, so this concept gives the traveller who wants to spend a longer period of time at a destination the best of both worlds (Talwani, 2007). Owners like the opportunity to have luxury accommodations that they can own, sell, or will to their heirs without dealing with the headaches involved with second home ownership.

'Fractional real estate sales were about $1.6 Billion in 2006 and are expected to continue to grow over the next several years. Most of these fractional real estate sales may be attributed to resort and niche fractional projects rolled out by large hotel operators, such as Four Seasons, St. Regis, and Ritz Carlton. With purchase prices for shares generally in the $200 000 to $1 Million range, these resort fractionals are positioned for the $200 000 plus per year household income purchaser' (Winter, 2008). Oftentimes, the fractionals will be constructed adjacent to a brand hotel so that they can share the same amenities and the developer will be better able to attain financing for the construction based on the monies collected from pre-construction fractional sales. There are independent as well as branded fractionals (private residence clubs); however, the brands tend to be more high profile in nature because of the brand identity associated with the product. In the next section, examples of fractionals that have expanded rapidly as part of a hotel brand will be presented in Tables 13.1–13.5.

Table 13.1 Four Seasons Residence Clubs
Services Offered
Fully furnished vacation home
With four seasons resorts setting with dining and amenities
Personalized owner services: pre-trip planning concierge, in-residence dining and housekeeping
Personal items stored: family photos and golf clubs, ski equipment will be waiting for the owner upon return.

Source: Four Seasons Residences, 2008

Table 13.2	Locations of Four Seasons Residence Clubs

Aviara, North San Diego, California, USA
Costa Rica at Peninsula Papagayo
Florence, Palazzo Tornabuoni, Italy
Jackson Hole, Wyoming, USA
Punta Mita, Mexico
Scottsdale at Troon North, Arizona, USA
Vail, Colorado, USA

Source: Four Seasons Residences, 2008

Table 13.3	St. Regis Residence Clubs, New York City, New York, USA

Services Offered and Size of Residences

Pressing service
Laundry service
Packing/unpacking service
24-Hour room service
Dining reservations
24-Hour security
Concierge service
Two bedroom 1183 square feet two bedroom two bath
One bedroom 804 square feet one bedroom one bath
Studio 430 square feet

Source: St. Regis Residences, 2008

Table 13.4	St. Regis Residence Clubs, Aspen, Colorado, USA

Services Offered and Size of Residences

A personal chef can be available at your request to cater every event from private dinners for two to more elaborate celebrations
The conveniences of top-of-the-line appliances including full sized refrigerator, stove, microwave, dishwasher and generous granite countertops for prepping
Concierge service
Favorite food and beverage stocked in residence by request
Ski clothing and equipment storage year round
24-Hour room service
Daily housekeeping with turn down service
Three bedroom approximately 2200 square feet
Two bedroom approximately 1700 square feet

Source: St. Regis Residences, 2008

Table 13.5	Ritz Carlton Clubs

Services Offered

Concierge service

Twice daily housekeeping

Lounges: Many sites include Club Members-only lounges where you can enjoy libations, light fare and the company of your fellow Members. These are especially popular gathering spots for groups of friends after a day on the links, the slopes or the beach.

Ski valet and golf concierge: at locations featuring skiing or golf professional attendants retrieve skis or clubs and set them up tune-up, clean and stow gear.

Member storage and pre-arrival residence set-up: Club Members are welcomed to leave their vacation wardrobes and any personal effects in their residences upon departure – including photographs, book and music collections, décor items and such. They are carefully packed and securely stored. Before the owner returns, the owners' clothes are cleaned and pressed and other things returned to the owners' residences, just as they left them.

Source: Ritz Carlton Clubs, 2008

DESTINATION CLUBS

Destinations Clubs are another spin off of the timeshare industry. They came on the scene in the 1990s and gained a great deal of media attention when Exclusive Resorts entered the picture in 2002 headed by American On-line co-founder Stephen Case. The concept of destination clubs is that it is a non-equity membership club. The member pays a membership/initiation fee and yearly dues and are given access to homes, villas around the world. The cost of the plans are based on the value of the homes in the club and the number of days in their membership. Most clubs have membership plans from ten up to sixty days a year. The cost is based on the number of days in each plan. The houses are rented or owned by the management company. The member does not own anything. Most clubs give back anywhere between 80-100% of their membership/initiation fee if the member chooses to get out of the club. The most popular reasons that people have chosen to join the Destination Clubs include the following (Destination Clubs, 2008b):

1. Cost-effective alternative to luxury hotels, villa rentals, fractional residences, and second home ownership.

2. Multi-location benefits.

3. No maintenance hassle and expenses.

4. Exclusive access to luxurious residences.

5. Three to five bedroom homes apt for larger groups.

6. Guaranteed access for a given number of days in a year.

7. Same high-end service of luxury resorts.

8. Concierge services for travel planning purpose.

9. Privacy.

10. Top-of-the-line furnishings.

Cost of plans

Because of the exclusive nature of destination clubs the homes are higher in value resulting a high monetary membership threshold. The membership deposits to join a club are included in Table 13.6:

Table 13.6 Membership Deposit Plans	
Ultra Luxury	$400,000 to $3,000,000
Luxury	$250,000 to $400,000
Moderate	$150,000 to $250,000
Value	$150,000 or less

Source: Destination Clubs (2008a)

The average membership deposit across all destinations clubs is $405,000 with the average value of each home where the members stay is $2.7 million. Based on the annual fees that are collected by destination clubs the average cost per night is $1,800 (Destination Clubs, 2008a).

Exclusive resorts

Exclusive Resorts is a destination club that was created in 2002 now they have more than 350 luxury residences (with over 120 more in development) around the world. Each residence averages three million dollars in value. Included in the residence is an Onsite Concierge that takes care of every vacation detail from stocking the pantry with the guests' favorite foods before their arrival to scheduling a private chef. The Onsite Concierge also plans any travel related excursion during their stay (For Example, restaurant reservations, show tickets, golf reservations). The residences also include a daily housekeeping service (Exclusive Resorts, 2008a).

Exclusive Resorts have residences around the world with different vacation experiences offered including 5 residences on the World cruise line (will be discussed later in the chapter. Tables 13.7–13.10 include the residences that are included in the Exclusive Resort club.

Table 13.7	Exclusive Resorts Beach residences

Anguilla, British West Indies
Bonita Beach, Florida
Ft. Lauderdale, Florida
Grand Cayman, Cayman Islands
Kapalua Bay, Maui, Hawaii
Kiawah Island, South Carolina
Kohala Coast, Big Island, Hawaii
Laguna Beach, California
Los Cabos, Mexico
Miami Beach, Florida
Peninsula Papagayo, Costa Rica
Real del Mar, Puerto Vallarta, Mexico
Rosewood Little Dix Bay, British Virgin Islands
Sea Island, Georgia
The Abaco Club, Bahamas
Turks & Caicos
Wailea, Maui, Hawaii

Source: Exclusive Resorts (2008b)

Table 13.8	Exclusive Resorts Mountain residences

Deer Valley, Utah
French Alps, France
Jackson Hole, Wyoming
Lake Tahoe, California
Snowmass, Colorado
Steamboat Springs, Colorado
Telluride, Colorado
Vail & Beaver Creek, Colorado
Whistler, British Columbia

Source: Exclusive Resorts (2008b)

Risk involved with destination club membership

The Destination Club membership is a non-equity arrangement so the members do not own anything which leads people to wonder what the inherent risks are in such an arrangement and how these risks are addressed by the management company. The reservation, membership deposit appreciation, and resignation risks will be analyzed in the following section (Destination Clubs, 2008a).

Table 13.9	Exclusive Resorts Metropolitan residences

Chicago, Illinois
Florence, Italy
Las Vegas, Nevada
London, England
New York, New York
Paris, France
San Francisco, California

Source: Exclusive Resorts (2008b)

Table 13.10	Exclusive Resorts Leisure residences

Bovey Castle, Devon, England
Carnegie Abbey Club, Newport, Rhode Island
Sailing aboard The World
Scottsdale, Arizona
Tucson, Arizona
Tuscany, Italy

Source: Exclusive Resorts (2008b)

Reservation risk

The clubs have the similar problem with the lodging industry in that peak seasons will attract many people to the same place. There are some clubs that include a certain amount of guaranteed access days with membership plans that will give them certain access to desired locations and times. Also, reservations are booked as far as year or months in advance which would be the most reliable way to ensure that the member received their desired time.

Membership deposit appreciation risk

Some members are concerned that they are losing money by placing such a large sum of money into a membership deposit. So to offset the concern that the club rather than the members are profiting from the real estate portfolio some clubs share in the real estate appreciation. At this point, however, these programs are relatively unproven.

Resignation risk

Members that want to resign from a club should receive the refundable portion of their membership deposit. Clubs usually have an agreement that two or three new members must join before receiving their monies back or setting a 12-18 month time limit to ensure the monies return to the ex-member.

Differences between fractionals and destination clubs

Fractional accommodations are usually condominium units that contain one to four bedrooms and are equipped with high-end furniture and fixtures. They are sometimes part of an exchange program and can go to different locations within the program. They are typically deeded pieces of real estate that owners can will to their heirs or sell. Some fractionals give the owner the opportunity to rent vacant time at their property. The owners pay a one-time purchase price and pay yearly assessments that take care of operating and maintaining the property (Weinberger and Kubick, 2008).

Destination club accommodations usually range from three to five bedrooms and are most often detached single-family homes with the exception of urban settings. They are also equipped with high-end furniture and fixtures. Destination Club members cannot rent their accommodations, but some programs allow you to share your membership with others for an extra cost (Weinberger and Kubick, 2008). Companies use this kind of program to become a member of a destination club and use their membership to give employees incentive travel vacations.

The destination club member pays a one-time membership initiation fee and pays yearly dues. They cannot sell their membership; however, as mentioned earlier in the chapter, most destination clubs have programs where the owner receives 80–100 per cent of their membership initiation fee back. They do not receive any of their yearly dues back (Weinberger and Kubick, 2008).

> **Key learning point 13.1**
> The evolution of the timeshare industry has expanded to a higher tier of vacationers seeking the luxuries of a second home without the hassle of upkeep and with choices around the world. The fractional and destination clubs have met this segment demand and continue to see growth.

CASE STUDY

Kevin and Bonnie Carver have heard about fractional and destination clubs through friends. Their interest peaked when they saw pictures of their friends' villas while on vacation. The Smith's have a great deal of liquid money, so the purchase will not be an investment opportunity in their eyes. They are looking to travel around the world with friends, staying in million dollar plus homes.

Residential cruise lines

The resident cruise industry is brand new with only one ship that is currently at sea and two others that are planned to set sail in 2010. The resident cruise industry serves the client that is looking to have access to luxurious accommodations year round or part of the year in an ownership capacity. This section will cover the current residential cruise offerings in this fledgling segment.

The appeal of the residential cruise industry is that a 43 000 ton cruise ship usually carries 1500–2000 passengers, but a residential cruise ship averages 285 guests per trip. A typical residence comes fully furnished with linen, china, crystal, and cutlery. The amenities may not be as abundant on a ship, with more passengers the residential cruises focus on the quality of the amenities offered as listed in Table 13.11.

Table 13.11   Amenities on Board Residential Cruise Ships

Movie theatres
Live stage shows
Nightclubs and bars
Casinos
Full-service spa
Gourmet grocery stores
Shopping – typically jewelry, fashion, and sundries
Fine dining-multiple restaurants, though the finest typically are open just a few
   nights per week
Tennis-on-board court and instructors
Golf-putting, chipping, driving range, golf simulators, pros and tee-times on land
Swimming – a variety of pools (including indoor) for exercise and relaxation
Fine wine available in restaurants or the guests' apartment from the ship's cellar
Gyms – individual and group fitness, open-air running track
Concierge services at every port that assists with land-based travel

Source: Halogen Guides (2008)

The owner has to pay a one-time purchase price as well as operating fees. The operating fee is collected monthly or quarterly and includes data in Table 13.12 (Halogen Guides, 2008).

Table 13.12	Operating Fee Covers

All Operating Expenses
May include dining under certain meal plans
Insurance for entire ship, including all public and private areas
Fuel
Crew
Port fees
Ship maintenance and repairs
Residence maintenance and repairs
Housekeeping, both public and private areas
Urgent medical care

Source: Halogen Guides (2008)

There are three companies that have a residential cruise line. The ResidenSea that operates the World that is currently at sea, The Four Seasons Ocean Residences (Four Season participation is as a licensing partner, they lent their name to Florida-based Ocean Development), and the Magellan. The profiles of the ships can be found in Table 13.13.

Table 13.13	Profiles of Current Ship Offers		
Ship Profile	**The World of ResidenSea**	**The Four Seasons**	**The Magellan**
Service date	2002	2010	2010
Decks	12	13	15
Rooms	165	112	212
Crew size	250	220	350
Suite configurations	1–6 Bedrooms	1–4 Bedrooms	1–4 Bedrooms

Source: Halogen Guides (2008)

The World of ResidenSea, The Four Seasons, and The Magellan all sell full ownerships, only The Magellan sells fractional, and The World of ResidenSea and the Magellan both have rental options (Halogen Guides, 2008). Financially, there is nothing similar to residential cruise ships to compare the purchase to at this point. What the owner is paying is real estate pricing for a depreciating asset with a finite lifespan. Each purchase for the three residential cruise ship companies is for a 50 year lease. There is a rental market for when the owner is not using their cabin; however, most owners consider it as a lifestyle purchase (Halogen Guides, 2008).

The Magellan (is set to sale in 2010) cabins will range in size from 624 to 2574 square feet. The fractionals that are being sold are as low as a two week use in a one bedroom cabin for $102 500 to $815 000 for a full month in a four bedroom penthouse. Full ownership in a one bedroom cabin would range from 2.5 million for a one bedroom cabin to 9.7 million for a four bedroom cabin. The operating expenses range from $3250 to $27 000 per year on fractional cabins and up to $324 000 a year for full ownership cabins. The ships' itinerary will include 300 unique destinations a year including Barcelona, New York, Sydney, Acapulco and Iceland during the course of ships two-year circuit around the globe (Balch, 2008).

Key learning point 13.2

The residential cruise line concept is an indication that consumers are beginning to embrace the ownership concept in all parts of their travel experience. The luxury cruise segment has been entered into and the success of this segment will most likely determine the entry into other cruise segments.

CASE STUDY

Pam and Ken Weaver are a retired couple and are looking to see the world. They have been avid boaters their entire life and considered selling their home and buying a yacht and sail around the world. Some friends mentioned the residential cruise line to the Weavers and thought that full ownership would be a better way to spend their retirement years in luxury seeing the world.

Reflective practice

1. Should the Weavers purchase a full ownership in a residential cruise line? What are the benefits? What are the downsides?

2. Do you think that residential cruise ownership will ever branch out from luxury cruises to mainstream cruises? Yes or no and why?

SUMMARY

What segment that will be the next evolution of the vacation ownership industry is a mystery. As this dynamic industry finds and attracts new market segments, the possibilities are limitless. The fractionals, destination clubs, and residential cruise lines are just in time for the babyboomers' retirement. So far, there is a great deal of interest in these high-end products and this will most likely continue to grow as long as the owners see high-end vacation ownership as financially viable. These experiences cater to the guest providing top of the line experiences that saves the owner time in vacation planning and maintenance.

References

AIF Toolkit (2008). American Resort Development Association International Foundation tool kit. http://www.arda.org/AM/Template.cfm?Section=AIF_ Toolkit1 retrieved on June 17, 2008.

AllEars.Net (2008). Disney Vacation Club: A primer. http://allears.net/acc/dvc. htm retrieved on May 1, 2008.

Alpander, G. (1991). Developing managers' ability to empower employees, *Journal of Management*, 10, 13–24.

Anderson, B.A., Povis, C., and Chappel, S.J. (2002). Coping strategies in the performance of emotional labour, Council for Australian University Tourism and Hospitality Education 2002 National Research Conference (CAUTHE), Perth.

Argenti, P.A. (1998). Strategic employee communications, *Human Resource Management*, 37/3–4, 199–206.

Aventuras Club (2008). A brief history of fractional and private residence clubs. http://condohotelcenter.com/articles/a121.htm retrieved on February 2, 2008.

Balch, L. (2008). High price tags on the high seas with new residential cruise line. Halogen Guides Real Estate. http://realestate.halogenguides.com/archives/ 1103-high-price-tags-on-the-high-seas-with-new-residential-cruise-line retrieved on April 2, 2008.

Barbee, C. and Bott, V (1991). Customer treatment as a mirror of employee treatment, *Advanced Management Journal*, 5/27.

Chin, Calvin. Helium report guide to condo hotels – part 1, Helium Report, April 16, 2007. Retrieved on Novermber 13, 2007

Collins (1993). *English Dictionary*, Glasgow: Harper Collins.

Condo hotels for second homes, vacation homes, retirement or investment (2007). http://www.condohotelcenter.com/articles/a4.html retrieved on November 16, 2007.

Conger, J.A. and Kanungo, R.B. (1988). The empowerment process: integrating theory and practice, *Academy of Management Review*, 13, 471–482.

Cooper, R. and Sawaf, A. (1997). *Executive EQ*, London: Orion Business.

Destination Clubs (2008a). Cost analysis. http://destinationclubs.org/cost-analysis retrieved on March 2, 2008.

Destination Clubs (2008b). Risk analysis. http://destinationclubs.org/risk-analysis retrieved on March 2, 2008.

Destination Clubs (2008c). Top benefits. http://realestate.halogenguides.com/destination-clubs retrieved on March 2, 2008.

Dial An Exchange. (2008). Dialanexchange.com retrieved on February 23, 2008.

Eaglen, A. and Lashley, C. (2001). *Benefits and Costs Analysis: The Impact of Training on Hospitality Business Performance*, Leeds: Leeds Metropolitan University.

Eaglen, A., Lashley, C., and Thomas, R. (2000). Modelling the benefits of training to business performance, *Strategic Change*, 9/4, 35–49.

Eaglen, A., Lashley, C., Thomas, R. (1999). *Benefits and Costs Analysis: The Impact of Training on Business Performance*, Leeds Metropolitan University: Leeds.

Exclusive Resorts (2008a). Activities and amenities. http://www.exclusiveresorts.com/#Activities_and_Amenities retrieved on March 2, 2008.

Exclusive Resorts (2008b). Site map. http://www.exclusiveresorts.com/SiteMap.html retrieved on March 2, 2008.

Fáilte Ireland (2005). *Strategy Statement 2005–2007*, Dublin: Fáilte.

Fineman, S. (1993) (ed), *Emotion in Organisations*, London: Sage.

Five-star living at condo-hotels in Miami, Boston, and San Francisco. (2004). *Investment Guide*.

Four Seasons Residences (2008). Four Seasons Residences home page. http://www.fourseasons.com/residences/ retrieved on March 31, 2008.

Germans embrace condo hotel concept in Miami: foreign investment in South Florida properties on the rise. (2007).

Goleman, D. (1998). *Working with Emotional Intelligence*, London: Bloomsbury.

Growth and development of timeshare industry. (2008). http://www.care-online.org/pospaper.html retrieved on January 11, 2008.

Halogen Guides (2008). *Decision Guide to Residential Cruise Ships*.

HEFCE (1998). *A Review of Hospitality*, London: Higher Education Funding Council.

Helium Report Guide to Condo Hotels (2007). http://www.heliumreport.com/archives/641-helium-report-guide-to-condo-hotels-part-1 retrieved on November 25, 2007.

Heslin, P.A.. (1999). Boosting empowerment by developing self efficacy, *Asian Pacific Journal of Human Resource Management*, 37/1, 52–65.

Hilton Grand Vacations Club (2008). http://www.hiltongrandvacations.com retrieved on May 1, 2008.

Hochschild, A.R. (2003). *The Managed Heart: Commercialization of Human Feeling*, Berkley: University of California Press.

http://www.condohotelcenter.com/articles/a45.html retrieved on November 23, 2007.

http://www.condohotelcenter.com/articles/a9.html retrieved on November 16, 2007.

International Cruises and Excursions. (2008). www.icegallery.com retrieved on March 13, 2008.

Interval International Public Relation Material (2007).

Johnson, P.R. (1993). Empowerment in the global economy, *Empowerment in Organisations*, 1/1, 13–18.

Jones, P., Koberg, C.S., Boss, R.W., Senjem, J.S., and Goodman, E.A. (1999). Antecedents and outcomes of empowerment: empirical evidence from the healthcare industry, *Group and Organization Management*, 24/1, 71–92.

Langhorn, S. (2004). *The Role of Emotion in Service Encounters*, DBA Thesis, University of Luton: Luton.

Lashley, C. (2000). *Hospitality Retail Management: A Unit Manager's Guide*, Oxford: Butterworth Heinemann.

Lashley, C. (2000a). Empowerment through involvement: a case study of TGI Friday's restaurants, *Personnel Review*, 29/5–6, 791–815.

Lashley, C. (2001). *Empowerment*: HR Practices for Service Excellence, Oxford: Butterworth Heinemann.

Lashley, C. (2004). Rhetorics and realities in hospitality and tourism employment practice: observations from some recent research projects, Conference Proceedings Tourism State of Art II, University of Strathclyde, Glasgow.

Lashley, C. and Morrison, A. (2003). Hospitality as a "commercial friendship", *Hospitality Review*, 6/3, 31–36.

Lashley, C., Best, W. (2001). Induction in licensed retailing, *International Journal of Contemporary Hospitality Management*, 14/1, 15–28.

Lashley, C., Morrison, A. and Randall, S. (2004). More than a service encounter? Insights into the emotions of hospitality through special meal occasions, *Journal of Hospitality and Tourism Management*, 12/1, 80–92.

Lashley, C., Rowson, W. (2000). Wasted millions: staff turnover in licensed retail organisations in Williams, A. (ed.) *Ninth Annual Hospitality Research Conference Proceedings*, University of Huddersfield.

Lashley, C., Thomas, R., and Rowson, B. (2002). *Employment Practices and Skill Shortages in Greater Manchester's Tourism Sector*, Leeds: Leeds Metropolitan University.

Leidner, R. (1993). *Fast Food, Fast Talk: Service Work and the Routinization of Everyday Life*, Berkley: University of California Press.

Lockwood, A., Baker, M., and Ghillyer, A. (1996). *Quality Management in Hospitality*, Cassell: London

Lynch, P.A. (2005). Reflections on the home setting in hospitality, *Journal of Hospitality and Tourism Management*, 12/ 1, 37–49.

Mahon, B. (1991). *Land of Milk and Honey*: *The Story of Traditional Irish Food and Drink*, Dublin: Poolbeg.

Mann, S. (1998). *Psychology Goes To Work*, Oxford: Purple House.

Mann, S. (1999). *Hiding What We Feel, Faking What We Don't*: *Understanding the Role of Emotions at Work*, Shaftsbury: Element.

Merrill Lynch (2007). Timeshare industry report. Merrill Lynch Industry Analysis report.

Morrissey, J. (2007). Homeowners embrace a unique arrangement: condo hotels and second homes. http://www.condohotelcenter.com/articles/a11.html retrieved on November 23, 2007.

Mullins, L. (2002). *Management and Organisational Behaviour*, London: Pitman

Nouwen, H. (1975). *Reaching Out*: *The Three Movements of the Spiritual Life*, New York: Doubleday and Co.

O'Gorman, K. (2006). Dimension of hospitality: exploring ancient and classical origins, in Lashley, C., Lynch, P., and Morrison A. (eds), *Hospitality: A Social Lens*, Oxford: Elsevier.

O'Mahony, B. (2003). Social and domestic forces in commercial hospitality provision: a view from Australia, *Hospitality Review*, 5/4, 37–41.

Orkin, Oren (2007). Financing your condo hotel unit. http://www.condohotelcenter.com/articles/a92.htm retrieved on November 16, 2007.

Orkin, Oren (2007). Financing your condo hotel unit. http://www.condohotelcenter.com/articles/a92.htm retrieved on November 16, 2007.

Parasuraman, A.., Berry, L.L., and Zeithaml, V.A.. (1991). Understanding customer expectations of service, *Sloan Management Review*, 32/3, 39–48.

Parson, S.G. (1995). Empowering employees – back to the future at Novotel, *Managing Service Quality*, 5/ 4, 16–21.

Pitt-Rivers, J. (2002). The laws of hospitality in Pitt-Rivers, J. (ed) *Essays in the Anthropology of the Mediterranean*, Cambridge: Cambridge University Press.

Podvin, S. and Pearsal, B. (2007). Latin Americans buyers spur development of condo-hotels in urban areas. http://www.condohotelcenter.com/articles/a1.html retrieved on November 23, 2007.

Potterfield, T.A.. (1999). *The Business of Empowerment*: *Democracy and Ideology in the Workplace*, Westport, CT: Quorum.

Putnam, L.L., and Mumby, D.K. (1993). Organisations, emotions and the myth of rationality, in Fineman, S. (ed), *Emotion in Organisations*, London: Sage.

Ragatz and Associates (2006a). A survey of non-buyers of resort timeshare,

Ragatz and Associates (2006b). Resort timeshare consumers: who they are, why they buy

Resort Condominiums International Public Relations Material (2007).

Resort Condominiums International (2008). www.rci.com retrieved on May 7, 2008.

Ritz Carlton Club (2008). Ritz Carlton Club home page http://www.ritzcarltonclub.com/ retrieved on March 31, 2008.

Ritzer, G. (1993). *The McDonaldization of Society,* London: Pine Forge Press.

Ritzer, G. (2002). *McDonaldization: The Reader,* London: Pine Forge Press.

Rodkin, D. (2004). Condo hotels move beyond resort towns. *The New York Times*, April 2, 2004, p. F8.

Rodwell, J.J., Kienzie, R., and Shadur, M.A.. (1998). The relationships among work-related perceptions, employee attitudes and employee performance: the integral role of communication, *Human Resource Management*, 37/3–4, 277–293.

St. Regis Residences (2008). St. Regis Residences home page. http://www.stregisresidenceclub.com/ retrieved on March 31, 2008.

Talwani, S. (2007). Taste of good life. Washington Diplomat. http://www.washingtondiplomat.com/September%202007/c2_09_07.html retrieved on December 12, 2007.

Taylor, F.W. (1947). *Scientific Management*, New York: Harper and Row.

Telfer, E. (2000). The philosophy of hospitality, in Lashley, C. and Morrison, A. (eds), *In Search of Hospitality: Theoretical Perspectives and Debates,* Butterworth Heinemann: Oxford.

The appeal of US property to foreign investors. (2007).What experts are saying. http://www.condohotelcenter.com/articles/a7.html retrieved on November 16, 2007.

Trading Places International (2008). www.tradingplaces.com retrieved on March 13, 2008.

Travel Industry of America (2008). Travelscope. http://www.tia.org/researchpubs/us_overview_trip_characteristics.html retrieved on May 4, 2008.

Vacation Ownership (2008). Frequently asked questions. http://www.vacationownership.com/pages/learn_faq.html retrieved on May 4, 2008.

Weinberger, M. and Kubick, D. (2008). Core differences between fractional ownership and a destination club membership. Halogen Guides Real Estate. http://realestate.halogenguides.com/archives/820-core-differences-between-fractional-ownership-and-destination-club-membership retrieved on July 24, 2008.

Winter, G. (2008). FSBO fractional: do-it-yourselfers beware. Sherpa Report. http://www.sherpareport.com/prc/fsbo-fractional.html retrieved on June 1, 2008.

Definition of Terminology

AMDETUR: (Asociacion Mexicana de Desarolladores Turisticos AC- Mexican Association of Resort Developers) The Mexican equivalent of ARDA.

Amenities: Features that enhance the value of the property such as swimming pools, tennis courts, golf courses, spas, boating, exercise centers, laundry facilities, etc.

ARDA: (American Resort Development Association) A major trade association in the United States for the timeshare industry. Provides lobbying and other services in support of the industry.

Bad Week: An interval that was previously viewed as usable and marketable that is no longer available for usage. This may be due to change of authorization of the owner of the interval, relinquishment of rights by owner to more than one party, duplication in the reservation system, or changes in the physical availability of the week.

Banking: Assigning usage of a week of timeshare with an exchange company.

Block (or Bulk) Banking: The depositing, usually by the resort management, of a large number of weeks with an exchange company.

Block Space: Inventory in which usage has been assigned or traded in which no specific traveler assignments have initially been designated.

Burn: Inventory that is not utilized and goes unoccupied. Many companies offer special travel promotions and price incentives as travel dates approach so as to avoid having inventory remain empty.

Cleaned and Pressed Inventory: Inventory in which the start dates, size, location, maintenance fees (if applicable) and owner authorization to occupy have been verified. This inventory is available to be exchanged, rented, or offered for rental.

Condo-Hotel: Portion of hotel room inventory sold to the public, which is typically deeded. Owners use for vacation or corporate housing needs or rent time that will not be utilized through a rental program managed by hotel.

CRDA (Canadian Resort Development Association): Not-for-profit national association serving the Canadian timeshare industry.

Destination Club: Fractional product that is not deeded. Involves the sale of memberships in an equity or non-equity club. Membership allows access in a network of resort homes in a variety of locations.

Exchange: The trade of one interval for another. Among companies, exchange means the trade of usage at one resort property for another. A fee is not normally charged if the exchange is between companies. Companies may consider seasonality, size and location when accepting a property in return for an offered property. An exchange can also occur when an individual owner transfers occupancy rights of their purchased interval to a company that specializes in exchange and pays an exchange fee to that company. An exchange can also be referred to as a trade or direct exchange or direct trade.

Exchange Company: A company or organization that accepts timeshare weeks on deposit from its interval owners or members to establish a pool of weeks from which other members may select the resort and vacation times of their choice.

Exit Program: Traditionally a reduced cost package/trial program offered to a customer who is at the point of walking away from a sales presentation. This helps recoup marketing costs and provides another opportunity for the resort to sell their property.

Fractional: Vacation ownership, usually a deeded interest, in a luxury vacation home for a predetermined time period. Exchange options are usually available to owners. Can be further defined as: Traditional Fractional interests, High- End fractional interests, Private Residence Clubs and Destination Clubs.

High End Fractional Interests (HFIs): Fractional product selling for $500 to $999 per square foot. Often characterized as "four star" quality.

Holiday Club/Vacation Club: A club that provides a number of weeks of vacation. These clubs are generally not covered by the laws regulating the sale of timeshare.

Interval: An assigned period of time. Based on the interval calendar wherein the fifty-two weeks of the year are numbered sequentially. A specific interval week is a seven-day period encompassing one of those fifty-two weeks.

Leased Inventory: Resort property that is not owned, but for which rights for usage have been contracted for and rented. Traditionally utilized in high demand areas where insufficient inventory has been released for exchange or company does not have access to exchange inventory. Many properties are receptive to annual or longer term leases so that revenue and usage are guaranteed. Many travel clubs, exchange companies or wholesalers lease inventory.

Maintenance Fee: Fees that are established and collected by the Homeowners Association or Resort Management Company to maintain property, pay insurance, utilities, refurbishing and taxes. The fees vary from resort to resort and with the type and size of the unit.

Management Company: The company contracted, usually by the Owners Association, to carry out the day-to-day management of the resort.

Marketing Company: A separate company from the developer responsible for marketing.

NACHO (National Association of Condo Hotel Owners): A non-profit trade association representing the entire life cycle of condo hotel segment from interested individuals and buyers, developers, supporting trades, and the individual unit owners.

One for One Exchange: Occurs when a determination has been made that no exchange balances will be outstanding. One company will relinquish usage of one piece of inventory only if acceptable inventory is offered as an immediate replacement. Companies may institute this policy when establishing a business relationship with a new company or invoke this policy when past trade balances have not been reconciled in a timely manner.

OTE (Organisation for Timeshare in Europe): The European equivalent of ARDA, but more consumer-oriented.

Points Conversion Program: An offering whereby owners of a timeshare week pay a fee to convert their timeshare ownership for the equivalent in points.

Private Resident Clubs (PRCs): Fractional product selling for $1,000 or more per square foot. Represent the pinnacle of quality with any resort accommodations available. "Five star" quality.

Rebook: To offer an alternate property or unit in lieu of a previously offered property.

Reconfirm: To contact directly the source of inventory or reservations office handling check-in to verify that the inbound traveler's name is noted on the reservation, the start date and size of unit is the same as noted on the written confirmation and the unit will be available to the traveler named on the confirmation for occupancy. This is normally done as a "double check" within one week of check- in dates. Reconfirm may also be referred to as "reverify".

Spacebanking: Depositing a week of owned timeshare with an exchange company.

TATOC (The Association of Timeshare Owners Committees): A non-profit association established in 1989 by a group of members representing timeshare resort owners committees throughout the United Kingdom, Ireland, Spain and Canary Islands, France, Portugal, Madeira and Austria. Currently recognized by the European timeshare industry as the only official voice for timeshare owners.

Three-way Exchange: A person or company that has occupancy rights to an interval assigns those occupancy rights to a second entity. The second entity then transfers those rights to a third entity. This process can be repeated numerous times, resulting in a four or five way exchange. Each entity that assigns usage is accountable to whom they have conveyed usage.

TIA (Travel Industry Association of America): A non-profit trade association that represents and speaks for the common interests and concerns of the entire U.S. Travel industry. It promotes increased travel to and within the United States through marketing initiatives and is the authoritative and recognized source of travel research.

Timeshare: A right, shared with others, to occupy a unit of accommodation for a period of time on a regular basis for a number of years.

Trade Balance(s): An accounting of intervals or weeks given to and received from one company to another. Internally, a company may review trade balances weekly. Trade balances among companies should be reconciled annually. Each company must determine acceptable trade balances based on nature of each business, past trade history and relationships, and availability of inventory.

Trading Power: The perceived value of an interval week when trading or exchanging for another week.

Traditional Fractional Interests: Product selling for less that $500 per square foot. Usually resort homes of average quality, with typical amenities and services. "Three star" level of quality.

Trial Membership: An ancillary product consisting of travel-related products and services, packaged with an opportunity to experience a developer's primary vacation ownership product within a defined period of time after the initial sales offering.

Unit Size: Normally expressed as hotel unit, studio unit and efficiency unit or number of bedrooms and maximum / minimum occupancy.

VRMA (Vacation Rental Managers Association): A professional trade association for the short-term property management industry.

Week 53: Almost all calendars contain only 52 weeks of use in a year, however, roughly every seven years there is an extra week which is referred to as week 53.

Wholesale: The discounted rental of a product. Rate is less than "rack rate". Companies or resorts typically offer inventory at wholesale rates in order to maximize inventory yield.

Source: C.A.R.E. *(Cooperative Association of Resort Exchangers)*

Index